D1598351

THE CLASSICS
OF **WESTERN**
SPIRITUALITY

THE CLASSICS OF WESTERN SPIRITUALITY
A Library of the Great Spiritual Masters

President and Publisher
Mark-David Janus, CSP

EDITORIAL BOARD

THE EARLIEST FRANCISCANS

The Legacy of Giles of Assisi, Roger of Provence, and James of Milan

Compiled and Introduced by
Paul Lachance, OFM, and Pierre Brunette, OFM

Translated by Kathryn Krug

Paulist Press
New York / Mahwah, NJ

Caseside art: Giotto di Bondone (1266–1336), *The Vision of the Chariot of Fire*. Fresco number VIII from the *Life of Saint Francis of Assisi* in the Basilica S. Francesco, Assisi. Photo credit: Scala / Art Resource, NY.

Caseside design by Cynthia Dunne, www.bluefarmdesign.com
Book design by Lynn Else

Library of Congress Cataloging-in-Publication Data

The earliest Franciscans : the legacy of Giles of Assisi, Roger of Provence, and James of Milan / compiled and introduced by Paul Lachance, OFM and Pierre Brunette, OFM ; translated by Kathryn Krug.
    pages cm
    Includes bibliographical references and index.
    ISBN 978-0-8091-0615-8 (hard cover : alk. paper) — ISBN 978-1-58768-495-1 (ebook)
    1. Franciscans—History—Sources. 2. Giles, of Assisi, -1262. 3. Roger, of Provence, -1309 or -1310. 4. James, of Milan, active 1238-1251. I. Lachance, Paul. II. Brunette, Pierre. III. Krug, Kathryn, translator.
    BV3606.3.E2713 2015
    271'.3022—dc23

BX
3606.3
.E2713
2015   2014035153

ISBN 978-0-8091-0615-8 (hardcover)
ISBN 978-1-58768-495-1 (e-book)

Published by Paulist Press
997 Macarthur Boulevard
Mahwah, New Jersey 07430

www.paulistpress.com

Printed and bound in the
United States of America

Contents

About the Contributors

PAUL LACHANCE, OFM, was born in Lewiston, Maine, and joined the Canadian Franciscan Province of Saint-Joseph, in Montreal, Canada. He lived his priesthood mostly in the USA. While doing manual labor and spiritual accompaniment, he lectured in Spirituality and preached retreats in the States and abroad. Fr. Lachance earned his doctorate at the Antonianum University of Rome with a dissertation on Angela of Foligno, on whom he wrote many articles and books. He taught Franciscan Spirituality and Mysticism at the Chicago Theologial Union and always pursued ministry with and advocacy for the poor, the elderly, and Latinos alongside his intellectual research. A regular participant and organizer of the Franciscan input at the International Congress of Medieval Studies of Kalamazoo, Fr. Lachance wrote prolifically on Franciscan Spirituality. He died in July 2011.

PIERRE BRUNETTE, OFM, was born in Ottawa, Canada, and joined the Franciscans in 1968. While earning his Master's degree in Pastoral Studies at the University of Montreal, he worked as a social worker in a poor neighborhood of the city. Ordained priest in 1979, Fr. Brunette was part of the Formation Team of his Province and later studied Spirituality at the Gregorian University in Rome, where he earned his doctorate with a dissertation on the writings of Saint Francis. While serving as Master of Novices in his Province and then as Minister provincial, he also lectured in France, Africa, Madagascar, and Peru. Fr. Brunette lives in the suburbs of Montreal, where he continues his research in Franciscanism and spiritual discernment, preaching, and ministry with the poor.

KATHRYN KRUG received a Master's degree in Medieval Studies from the University of Chicago. Her translations of Medieval and Renaissance Latin appear in books published by the University of Chicago Press, where she served as manuscript editor. During this time she also taught Latin in the non-credit program of the Hyde Park Cluster of Theological Schools. She has worked with Fr. Lachance and Fr. Brunette on Francis of Assisi and His Conversions, translating Fr. Lachance's French original into English, and she collaborated for many years with Fr. Lachance in his work on Angela of Foligno. Mrs. Krug is now engaged in freelance editing and translation, including a translation of twelfth-century sermons of Aelred of Rievaulx (in progress).

ACKNOWLEDGMENTS

As we look back at the journey that led to the completion of this book, it would have seemed more than relevant to let Father Paul Lachance, Franciscan, take a stand, explain the origins of the project, and acknowledge the contribution of so many people. His premature death in 2011 narrowed down our book anthology to more humble goals. This volume is thus dedicated to Paul's memory, to his wonderful scholarly work in the field of Franciscan spirituality and mysticism.

It would have been Paul's wish to thank his close friend, mentor, and colleague Bernard McGinn for his insights and counsels along the way. I wish to extend my warm gratitude to Professor McGinn and his wife, Pat, for the expertise and support that enabled me to put closure to the initial project. *The Earliest Franciscans* would never have seen the light of day without him. Bernie opened us to the exceptional world of Roger of Provence many years ago.

My immense gratitude goes to Kathryn Krug, who painstakingly checked the drafts of the texts many times over; her editorial and literary skills added fidelity to her translation of the Latin original. The outcome of her contribution renders beauty and, most of all, clarity to sometimes obscure devotional and mystical passages. Even before the death of Paul Lachance, Kathy's commitment to the project established her as a precious collaborator.

Finally, Paul would have wanted to express his gratitude to the many friends who shared with him the discoveries made while working with the chosen medieval authors. Some have proofread parts of our texts; others have reacted to the spiritual insights triggered by the profound wisdom and imagery of the texts: David Burr, Michael Cusato, OFM, Jane Davidson, Sister Pacelli Millane, OSC, Colette Wisnewski, and many more. To each one of them, and to the countless students and companions of Paul during his journey, especially the brothers of our Canadian Province of Saint Joseph, thank you for helping us add our *little stone* to the Franciscan legacy.

Pierre Brunette, OFM

General Introduction

"Who are these men," asks Lady Poverty, "who fly like clouds and like doves to their windows? It has been a long time since I have seen such people or gazed upon those so unencumbered, all their burdens set aside."[1]

An Uneasy Questioning

This book project was inspired by some passages like the one above in the *Sacrum Commercium—The Sacred Exchange between Saint Francis and Lady Poverty* (1237–39),[2] relevant to the Franciscan crisis that erupted long before Francis's death in 1226. It involved more than the passionate discussions on poverty that were later centered around the debate of the *Usus Pauper*.[3] Many issues at the core of the "identity crisis" were related to the too-rapid growth of the Order.

Francis resigned as Minister General of the Friars Minor in 1220. Several unsolved issues appeared later on; they could not have been foreseen during the composition of the *Rule* (1221–23). For example,

The acceptance into the Order of candidates coming from different walks of life, raising questions of formation, work, and occupations, and the growing value of studies.[4]

The shift from itinerancy to a more settled way of life, involving landownership, building projects, libraries, and study centers.[5]

The increased complexity of the daily necessities of a growing population.[6]

The organizational demands of a blossoming institution that started out as a group of local companions, and the changing face of its leadership.[7]

The need for new modes of Franciscan presence in an urban context marked by the communal movement and the call to go beyond the borders of Italy.

A constant process of discernment due to a rapid transformation in the mendicant life and its community settings. Tensions arose among the friars regarding whether it was better to live in the wilderness far from city life, or in small friaries, or even in bigger convents closer to the people.[8]

The emergence of pastoral ministries in the hands of the friars giving access to coveted positions and bringing fame and privileges.[9]

These are problems at the core of the "identity crisis" of the flowering Order. Ten years after its foundation, more than five thousand friars were counted. During the French Revolution, the list exceeded 100,000. No other church group had developed so rapidly and produced such an impact outside its ranks. Yet from the time of its approval by the papacy in 1209, structural issues mingled with the constant challenge of faithfulness to the original *forma vitae*: the call to radical gospel discipleship in fraternity.

These problems, in time, gave way to key witnesses, opposing factions, fierce debates, and unofficial currents of thought. The famous *question franciscaine*, dealing with the authority of Franciscan hagiography, revealed more than a search for the true identity of Francis of Assisi; it also concerned the identity of the changing face of the Brotherhood. With the exception of the *First Life of Francis*, written by Thomas of Celano in 1228, the other Franciscan *Lives* or *Legends* tried to resolve the identity crisis from within the Order and respond to this ongoing question: What is a Friar minor?[10]

In the *Sacred Exchange*, quoted above, Lady Poverty pursues her inquiry about a category of friars able *to ascend in haste to the top of the mountain*—one understands to the summit of a radical gospel life:

She addresses these friars: "What is the reason for your coming and why have you come so quickly from the valley of misery to the mountain of light? Are you perhaps looking for me who, as you see, am a poor little one tossed about by storms and without consolation?"[11]

Reading between the lines, it is obvious that some friars were seen as champions capable of risking the ascent to perfection and, at the same time, a majority of friars were questioning the basic principles of such a radical way of living. Later in the text, Lady Poverty castigates the friars unfaithful to their calling: "When there was a cessation of persecution among my children, war, domestic and internal, tears them apart with greater cruelty. They envy one another and provoke one another in acquiring riches and luxuriating in delights."[12]

The *Sacred Exchange* draws a stark picture of the impostors opposing Lady Poverty while she clings stubbornly to the past. They say, "May the poverty you seek always be with you, your children, and your seed after you. As for us, however, let it be our good fortune to enjoy delights and to abound in riches, for the duration of our lives is tedious and demanding."[13]

These excerpts take us back to a more political stance of Francis in his dictation on *True and Perfect Joy*. At the end of his life, Francis rejects as a source of personal joy the entrance of prestigious candidates into the Order, such as the masters of Paris, the brilliant prelates, bishops, and kings from afar. He also turns down, as a reason to rejoice, the conversions of nonbelievers and miracles accomplished by the Brotherhood. He depicts, rather, his own trial in front of his peers, relying on patience and perseverance, as the source of true joy. This painful narrative, endured for the love of God, expresses bluntly the rejection of his leadership, his loss of grip over a successful Order, and most of all, the refusal of his person and the lifestyle he represented as a lay unlearned man. Brother Francis felt reduced to nostalgia by his peers, like an outcast among his own: "Go away! This is not a decent hour to be wandering about!...Go away! You are simple and stupid! Don't come back to us again! There are many of us here like you—we don't need you!...Go to the Crosiers' place and ask there."[14] The experience is both spiritual and political, but one interprets also his parable as the discontent of a majority of friars regarding the origins of the Order.

These questions and reproaches display an increasing tension in the Brotherhood. The heritage left by Francis and his early companions seems to have been difficult to pursue. The *Sacred Exchange*, as well as the parable on *True and Perfect Joy*, launched the *The Earliest Franciscans* project in Father Paul Lachance's mind a few years ago.[15] It seemed obvious to him that some friars wanted to carry on the insights of the Franciscan beginnings until the end of the fourteenth century. Their strong evangelism appeared paradoxically as loyalty and rebellion: loyalty to the Founder and resistance toward the evolution of the Order.

"Who Are These Men?"

A number of friars fit Lady Poverty's definition of men like "flying clouds and doves." They receive no recognition whatsoever from a majority of friars. "These men" are neglected by scholars because they have never created theological currents or schools or produced important *Summas*. A few remain confined to the field of vernacular teachings, popular devotion, or extreme mystical experiences. Yet they reveal themselves as true witnesses of the Franciscan message without being masters in theology, saintly preachers, or instigators of disciples. Their originality resists classification. First associated to a movement of resistance, some get identified with the Spiritual wing of the Order. Their strong opinions and behavior and, most of all, their unquestionable attachment to Francis's legacy ignites provocation. A common denominator binds these men together: their passion for the Founder's evangelism.

The Earliest Franciscans project originally selected three categories of authors who illustrate their fidelity to the *forma vitae* and the development of Christian perfection as initiated by Francis and his companions.

1. Witnesses of the first generation (Giles, Leo and Clare of Assisi, Roger of Murcia, and some excerpts from the *Sacred Exchange*).

2. Authors concerned with Christian growth and perfection (Roger of Provence, James of Milan, David of Augsburg, Guibert of Tournai, and the *Meditatio pauperis in solitudine*).

3. Brothers identified as leaders of the Spirituals (Peter Olivi, Ubertino of Casale, and Angelo Clareno).

Needless to say, the amplitude of the project and the many differences between the writings and the lives of these men were daunting. As mentioned previously, and because of Father Paul Lachance's premature death, our choice of authors finally narrowed down to three Franciscans: Giles of Assisi, Roger of Provence, and James of Milan—and, time allowing, mentions of other works, such as a neglected chapter of Ubertino of Casale's *Arbor Vitae*.

These men come from regions in which the Spirituals had a strong impact: the Umbrian valley, the region of Provence, Lombardy, and Tuscany. Each one passes on something of the Franciscan experience, whether through controversial actions, strong spiritual convictions, disconcerting mystical experiences, or even severe statements on religious life. Their influence over the Brotherhood and the secular Franciscans is undeniable.

The uniqueness of these men transcends any scholastic model. Their words and deeds prove they are more than "free doves," or a bunch of unsettled friars.[16] One cannot tag them as dissidents without naming their reluctance to any softening of the *forma vitae* or any change in the Order. Franciscan history and theology still does not know how to evaluate their contribution to the movement, typecasting them as rebels on the fringe of the community.

The Earliest Franciscans wishes to voice their spirituality with its specific accents in the Franciscan thirteenth- and fourteenth-century literature. Paul Lachance used Lady Poverty's questioning as a framework for our research: Who are these men? What is their legacy regarding the *forma vitae*? What main accents mark their mysticism, their spirituality, and their theology? What is missing or neglected in their work? Why is their contribution to the Franciscan legacy a difficult one?

A Patchwork of Spiritual Writings and Life Narratives

The small collection of works published here displays many literary genres. From Giles of Assisi, in his *Golden Words* or *Sayings*, we have numerous teachings communicated orally, then dictated or reported by a secretary (*verba dicta, verba dictata,* and *verba reportata*). The content of his *Sayings* ranges from ascetical essays on vices and virtues to admonitions on religious life, and especially, thoughts on contemplation acquired through authentic mystical experiences. His genre resembles that of the pungent and exhortatory *Apophthegmas* of the Desert Fathers and Mothers. Giles represents the first disciples of Francis without schooling, just like Leo and Clare of Assisi. Leo's writings, *The Writings of Leo, Rufino and Angelo, Companions of St. Francis* (*Scripta Leonis, Rufini et Angeli Sociorum S. Francisci*) and his *Intentio regule,* and Clare's *Privilege of Poverty* (*Privilegium paupertatis*) and *Letters to Agnes of Prague* emphasize the importance of the Franciscan *Rule* and *Testament* as much as Giles's *Sayings.*[17]

Roger of Provence produced forty compact *Meditations* with the aid of his daily companion and confessor. His spiritual reflections take the form of exhortations on matters of the soul, and on the constant search for divine realities. He is closest to Francis's vision of God's unfathomable presence. The content of his teaching reaches religious men and women outside his close network of friars.

James of Milan continues in the same vein: his *Stimulus amoris* or *Goad of Love* is a devotional work that intertwines profound meditations, dense mystical prayers, and flights of poetry with ascetical treatises and moral teachings, for the sake of the soul in search of God and ready to identify with the suffering Christ.

Both Roger and James represent a more literate category of authors, close to the *Vade mecum* genre, like David of Augsburg's writing *On the Interior and Exterior Person* (*De exterioris et interioris hominis compositione*), Guibert of Tournai's *Essay on Virginity* (*Tractatus de virginitate*), John Peckam's *Song of the Poor* (*Canticum pauperis*), and the popular *Meditation of a Poor Person in Solitude* (*Meditatio pauperis in solitudine*).[18] All of the above reveal their fascination for the challenge of personal spiritual growth and perfection, and because of that, they are often associated with the current of the Spirituals.

Once in contact with the richness of the chosen authors' writings, we felt the need to complete our documentation with brief biographical narratives, providing a secondary source collected from reliable confidants. Facts from their lives gave access to their personality, revealing their strengths and their flaws, and the balance between how they write and how they live. We can thus identify their contribution to Franciscan spirituality: their words and deeds serve the cause of gospel life. Giles, Roger, and James stand as true witnesses of the Franciscan legacy, by their example as much as with their writings.

I

GILES OF ASSISI

Mystic and Rebel

Introduction

Coming from peasant stock, Giles was the third of the early companions of Francis of Assisi, after Bernard of Quintavalle and Pietro Cattani. He was born in Assisi around 1190 and joined Francis at the Portiuncula on April 23, 1209. He was one of the twelve who, in the spring of 1209, went with Francis to Rome to receive the approval of the first *forma vitae* of the Friars Minor from Pope Innocent III. He also accompanied Francis on his early missions. Giles is remembered mostly for his pithy and pungent *Sayings*—three hundred or so—reminiscent, in style and spirit, of the *Admonitions* of Francis and the *Apophthegma* of the Desert Fathers.[1]

The other main sources for information about Giles are the three *Vitae* or *Lives*, each with its distinctive characteristics: the so-called *Short Life*, fairly recently edited by Rosalind Brooke;[2] the *Long Life*, which is a more comprehensive compilation of texts of varying value and is to be found in the early fourteenth-century Franciscan source titled *Chronicle of the Twenty-Four Generals*;[3] and a third one, similar to the latter and unfairly considered of lesser importance.[4] All three *Lives* are ascribed to Brother Leo, a close friend of Giles who outlived him for nine years and who, like him, was an early and very close companion of Francis. Because of these sources, the *Dicta* in the critical edition and in four surviving collections and the *Vitae*, along with the many references to Giles in other early Franciscan hagiography,[5] we are in a position to know more about him than about any of Francis's other early companions.[6]

As for the *Dicta*, at present the main source is the critical edition prepared by Gisbert Menge, OFM, in 1905.[7] The spiritual richness of some of these *Dicta* notwithstanding, reading them in this edition or translations thereof can be at times tedious and uninspiring. Thematically organized into twenty-six chapters, the *Dicta* often come across as more concerned with the practice of ascetical and moral virtues, some with a dualistic bent, than as having much if any bearing on the evolution of the early Franciscan movement or, for that matter, shedding much clarity on the nature of contemplation.

We are thus faced with a conundrum when we try to come up with a picture of who Giles really was. On the one hand, in the official sources, Celano and Bonaventure's *Lives* of Francis, Giles is mentioned as a model of early Franciscan life. Hardly anything is said about his fraternal and social involvements and his daily activities. Moreover, these sources tend increasingly to idealize and encapsulate Giles into the role of a mystical person who lived in seclusion and did not have any direct impact, or so it would seem, on the early Franciscan movement. On the other hand, the authors or compilers of mostly nonofficial sources, some of which will also be indicated in what follows, not only highlight Giles's contemplative gifts but also, likely amplifying and annotating his words and actions, present him as a mouthpiece for the criticism of the evolution of the Order. The solution, then, is elusive and calls for an exercise in intertextuality—that is, mixing and matching the various layers of the tradition concerning Giles with what we can know otherwise of the primitive Franciscan ideal and its turbulent early heritage. Important clarification can certainly be brought about by contextualizing the *Dicta* as well as the deeds and stories concerning Giles and, whenever possible, locating their *Sitz im Leben*, not only as they appear in the *Vitae* but also in the various nonofficial Franciscan sources and compilations: the *Leonine Corpus*, now more or less amalgamated in the *Compilatio Assisiensis*, *The Chronicle of the Twenty-Four Generals*, the *De Conformitate* of Bartholomew of Pisa, the Salimbene and Eccleston *Chronicles*, and finally, the writings of two of the leaders of the Spirituals, Ubertino of Casale and Angelo Clareno, who made Giles one of their champions.

To help make our way through this maze, it is also important to note that the *Dicta*, along with brief theological treatises and polemical tracts, are part of a current of writings that finds its source in the hermitages and popular preaching. They were meant to defend and transmit the primitive Franciscan ideal outside of the established forms and canons. Furthermore, the composition of the *Dicta* follows a trajectory identical to that of the *Admonitions* of Francis. In both cases, the collation of their statements is done while the protagonists are still alive. Their oral transmission precedes the written form and, in the case of the *Dicta,* begins around 1224 and continues until a more definitive text is established toward the end of the thirteenth century. Whether and to what extent these *Dicta* are the very words, the *ipsissima verba,* of Giles is impossible to determine at this stage of research. Moreover, as with Francis's *Admonitions,* close affinity also exists between the *Dicta* of Giles and the *Apophthegmata* of the Fathers and Mothers of the desert.

It is a well-documented but neglected fact that when the brothers assembled in chapter, reference to the *Lives of the Desert Fathers* was a constant practice.[8] There existed an oral tradition of Franciscan maxims, grafted onto the ancient monastic source.[9] The medieval forests had replaced the desert as the place for spiritual combat, and out of wild and remote settings, often in question-and-answer format, the early Franciscan hermits such as Giles would forge their concise and provocative sayings and opinions, not only concerning spiritual life, but also on many of the questions being debated in the Franciscan movement since the death of Saint Francis.[10] In short, it is the contextualizing of the *Dicta,* whenever possible, combined with what we can know through the *Vitae* and the aforementioned chronicles, that can shed some light on the brother whom Francis hailed as one of his very special "knights of the Round Table."[11]

Our brief presentation of this archetypal Franciscan and fool of God will follow the lead of his biographical profile, which can be summarized with the dominant motifs of each period as follows: from 1209 to 1215: the disciple and pilgrim; from 1216 to 1226: the itinerant and visionary; from 1227 to 1239: the dissident; from 1240 to 1262: the influential hermit and mystic; and in conclusion, the final years.

From 1209 to 1215: The Disciple and Pilgrim

We have practically no information on Giles before 1209, concerning his youth or his family. The tradition speaks of his poor origins. Coming from peasant stock, he is presented as "simple and unlettered,"[12] a layperson of no importance. His great physical strength enables him to be a hard and tireless manual laborer. Celano's *First Life* describes him as "a simple upright man who feared God."[13] Just a few years later, the early biographies remember his fidelity, piety, and the graces of contemplation he received.[14] Bonaventure, in the *Legenda Major*, specifies that he should be taken as a model of the perfect contemplative: he "was raised to the height of exalted contemplation."[15] And later still, it will be said of him that he was "filled with the gift of the Holy Spirit," or even "wounded by the Holy Spirit."[16]

Giles was eighteen years old when, on the feast of St. George, he joined the first friars at St. Mary of the Angels, the cradle of the Franciscan movement. He expressed his radical break from the world by taking off his shoes and giving his cloak to a poor woman importuning him.[17]

Giles shared the minority ideal of Francis and the early brotherhood: a life of contemplation and penury inspired by the poverty of Christ, and marked by itinerancy, manual labor, and sharing the condition of the poor. He is quoted as saying, "Love poverty to have the strength to imitate the poor Christ and to be able to be more freely available for God."[18] He was especially ingenious at finding odd jobs to perform. By turns, he worked as a water carrier, gravedigger, olive picker, basket weaver, and nurse to lepers, and at other forms of manual labor. He had such a strong personality and independent spirit that Francis gave him free rein to do what he pleased for approximately fifteen years, during six of which Giles wandered to faraway places. This freedom of movement is what explains his many travels and long pilgrimages to the main shrines of the times: St. James at Compostela, St. Michael at Gargano, St. Nicholas at Bari, and the sanctuaries in Rome and in the Holy Land.[19] During his travels, through his words and actions, manual labor, and begging, he served as an exemplar of the early Franciscan ideal. Giles was also the one who accompanied Francis in his very first preaching mission to the Marches, as well as one of the first brothers who followed Francis to Rome in order to obtain the initial approval for the *forma vitae* from Pope Innocent III.

In 1213 Giles predicted the future tribulations of the Brotherhood, the first negative prophecy of the outcome of the Franciscan movement to be found in the early legends.[20] He also wanted, henceforth, to be under obedience, since "his conscience [was] unable to find rest"[21] with the freedom at his disposal. Thus, Francis sent him to the hermitage of Fabriano on the Perugian plain, then to the fraternity near the church of St. Apollinaris in Spoleto. There, pursuing a life of prayer, penance, and poverty, Giles experienced his first visions,[22] each of which was accompanied by strong trials and assaults from the devil.[23] The Lateran Council of 1215 forbade laypersons to preach, and this edict helped prompt Giles to find moments to withdraw and live in seclusion. Francis increasingly noticed how special he was and singled him out as one of his brothers "who conceal themselves in remote and desert places that they may more diligently apply themselves to prayer and meditation, and weep over the sins of themselves and others. Their holiness is known to God, though it may be unknown to the friars and to [other] people."[24]

From 1216 to 1226: The Itinerant and Visionary

What we know of Giles's early ecstatic experiences, as just noted, is that they likely took place during the time he spent in hermitages when not traveling. This was during the heyday of the missionary expansion of the burgeoning Franciscan movement, and Giles shared this missionary motivation.[25] In 1219 chroniclers concur that Giles boarded ship for Tunisia, where he wanted to die as a martyr.[26] In one of his *Dicta*, he laments that the five Franciscans who died as martyrs in Morocco were not canonized, and he evokes their memory: "If we had not had the example of the Fathers who have gone before us, perhaps we would not be in the state of repentance we are in now."[27] When he returned to Italy a short time later, Umbria became his favorite place of residence. Then in 1224, in the Rieti valley for a while, he was the guest of Cardinal Chiaramonti.[28] His radicalism drew followers to his side. With one of these new companions, he settled in Deruta for the Lent of 1226. In the same year, on October 3, he was at the bedside of the dying Francis, and the *Legend of Perugia* even has Francis blessing him, instead of Bernard, as in other accounts.[29]

It is significant to note that shortly after the death of Francis, Giles changed his life radically and was impelled to deepen his search for God by more prolonged periods of living alone in hermitages. From then on, for more than thirty-five years, we see him going from hermitage to hermitage in the Perugian valley. In 1226, beginning three days before Christmas, at Cetona in Chiusi, an intense period of visions and mystical states took place that had a determinative effect on the rest of his life. In Leo's account, Francis appeared to Giles in his sleep, counseling him to "be attentive to himself." Shortly thereafter, visions of Christ happened. Giles describes the effects of these visions as "being inundated day and night with a most agreeable scent and sweetness of heart so intense that he can hardly bear it." These powerful experiences of divine presence continued until Epiphany.[30] They were so powerful that he referred to them as a trial suffered by another person, modeling his style on St. Paul: Giles "knows of a man whose vision of God was so clear that he had lost all faith."[31] The fullness of these visions was as if he did not need faith anymore.

Diabolical temptations came with these visions, however, and threw him into such a state that he let out screams so loud as to greatly alarm his brothers, who thought he was dying.[32] Giles, for his part, insisted on his unworthiness and averred that he was just a sinner, an ordinary man, an uneducated peasant. To a brother at his side, he even disclosed that "he experiences himself as an enemy of God" and doubted "whether he is working in accordance with God's will," fearful that "some people may ask of him what he cannot give to them." When these ecstatic moments were over, Giles was heard saying, "As God breathed on the Apostles, even so he has breathed on me."[33]

It is important to note that these visionary experiences, and Giles's refusal to speak about them, are in keeping with many of Giles's *Dicta* that speak about the necessity for silence, reticence, and indirection in speaking about mystical experiences.[34] Out of concern, then, to keep the graces he has received from God jealously to himself, Giles would henceforth create greater distance between himself and others, including his own brothers. He is quoted as saying, "One must be alone and free to devote oneself to God and to one's soul. For the Lord alone, who created the soul, is its friend and no one else."[35] His solitary life during more than thirty-five years was the consequence, then, of a personal choice ensuing, mainly, from the raptures he went through at Cetona.

We must situate in this period the famous Saying "On Contemplation" found in the *Dicta*.[36] Giles is recorded as responding to an inquiry concerning contemplation by distinguishing seven stages emphasizing the progressive action of the spiritual senses: *fire, anointing, ecstasy, contemplation, taste, rest,* and *glory.* The text is Giles's most important contribution to mystical theology because of its roots in Pseudo-Dionysian thought and its influence on later tradition. Thomas Gallus, a French theologian and member of the school of St. Victor, also a pivotal figure in medieval mysticism, refers to Giles's Saying "On Contemplation" in a treatise of 1224. Studies show that Gallus had been acquainted with the text through his friendship with Anthony of Padua.[37] Thanks to Giles, Gallus had a strong influence on Franciscan, Benedictine, and Carthusian authors from the thirteenth to the sixteenth centuries. The same chapter on contemplation will also inspire Bonaventure twice in his own writings.[38]

After this decade of itinerancy, solitude, and intense visions, it becomes difficult to follow Giles's life very closely. What we know of it fades into the crevices of the official accounts of what is taking place in the Franciscan movement at the time: problems of leadership, organization, expansion, and clericalization, and attempts to interpret or adapt the Rule to new situations and the resistance to these efforts. From 1226 onward, the official Franciscan hagiographical legends—those that form the dominant culture—eliminate Giles from the important events taking place in the fraternity. Relegating Giles to the contemplative life and out of circulation strategically serves the leadership of the Community faction in the Order by discouraging the minority of Spirituals. Giles, for his part, was one of the hardliners who called for an application, without gloss, of the heritage of Francis.[39] What seems to be a break from the world, an *exire de seculo,* in favor of withdrawal, needs also to be understood as a political statement against the adaptations and compromises proposed by the Community faction. Zealous rigorists such as Giles protest against any "softening" of the initial gospel ideal.

From 1227 to 1239: The Dissident

The chronology during this period is more and more fractured and gets lost in approximations. Giles wandered from Spoleto to

Agello, Assisi, and Perugia. This was the period of the generalate of John Parenti (1227–32) and the second mandate of Elias of Cortona as the head of the Order (1232–39). Giles openly opposed the construction by Elias of the large convent in Assisi and the basilica honoring Francis. His position would incite Leo and a small band of resisters to smash the marble box used to collect the building funds. Giles could not stand the betrayal of the commitment to poverty.[40] During his first generalate, from 1220 to 1227, Elias had denounced the excessive autonomy to the disciples of "the first hour," their vagabond ways, and their break with holy obedience to Pope Gregory IX.[41] But at the end of his second term, some of these very same accusations would return to be leveled against him and eventually lead to his being deposed by the pope in 1239. Giles, for his part, when he heard about the downfall of Brother Elias, his disobedience, apostasy, and excommunication, prostrated himself on the ground, pressing his whole body tightly to the earth. Asked why he was doing this, he replied, "I want to get down as low as I can. The higher one leaps, the farther one falls."[42]

Giles was also a fierce opponent of studies: "Do not put your confidence in your knowledge."[43] In his opinion, knowledge was of no use without works and deeds. He would also be portrayed accosting a brother preacher with a sarcastic gesture, placing two fists before his mouth to represent a trumpet and, in his Umbrian dialect, telling him that instead of his sermon he should shout out, "Bo, bo, molto dico, poco fo!" (I talk a lot but do little).[44] As for the Franciscan scholars with inflated egos teaching at the University of Paris and diluting the demands of the Rule, Giles berated them by shouting, "Paris, Paris, you are destroying the Order of St. Francis."[45] In his opinion, the Order was in a state of total ruin: "The ship is wrecked. The battle is lost," he cried out, "let those who can run, run, and escape if they can."[46] Ubertino of Casale reports that he wept so loudly over the destruction of the practice of the Rule that the young friars entering the fraternity thought he was insane. Jesus had to come in a vision to reassure Giles that the Order will eventually be renewed and observance of the Rule will be restored.[47] One of Giles's *Dicta* will identify the cause for such a bad state of affairs: "Many are entering religion without practicing what is appropriate for the religious state."[48]

As for Francis, Giles held him in great esteem. Asked once what to make of Blessed Francis, he responded excitedly, "That man Francis ought never be named without smacking one's lips for joy. Only one thing was lacking to him: physical strength. If he had had a strong body like mine, I am certain the whole world put together would not have had the strength to follow him."[49] In one of the Cetona visions, Francis even appeared to him and told him "to be attentive to himself."[50] But, as previously noted, even at the beginning Giles had already manifested his independent spirit by long periods not spent in Francis's presence, either on long pilgrimages or in hermitages. In later years, he became even more detached and critical. He seemed at one point to be very uncomfortable with the cult that was growing around Francis because of the vision and the stigmata the latter had received at Mount La Verna. To one brother who mentioned how great this event had been and asked him about it, he curtly replied, "My son, no creature can be compared with the Creator,"[51] and later on to the same question posed by another brother, Giles responded apophatically, "Those things were great, but the works of the Lord are one thing, and He himself is something else."[52] Pressed further on the subject of mystical experiences, he said, "If I glorify myself, my glory is nothing," and added, "Let us not say any more about this."[53]

From 1240 to 1262: The Influential Hermit and Mystic

In this part of his life, "holy brother Giles," as he is often called in the various accounts, increasingly acquired the reputation of being a holy man and a mystic.[54] Three companions joined him: Gratian, Andrew, and John. It was also in this time that John of Parma was elected Minister General of the friars. His election was greeted with enthusiasm by Leo, Angelo, Masseo, and even Giles— all companions of Francis—because it seemed to them that St. Francis "had been resurrected in spirit" in friar John. Giles, nonetheless, sounded a warning note: "It is good and fitting that you have come, but you have come too late," so convinced was he that it was now too late for the Order to return to the purity of its early years.[55]

Important leaders of the Church and the Order, such as the pope (Gregory IX), various prelates, Bonaventure, and Lady Jacoba (Francis's Roman friend) filed up to visit Giles in his hermitage of

Monteripido in Perugia. During this period, he would also keep contact with Francis's first companions, Clare and the Damianites.[56]

In 1253, coinciding with the construction of the basilica in Assisi, Celano's *Treatise on Miracles* appeared, with its eulogy of Francis. According to Ubertino of Casale, Giles once again manifested his opposition to such a display of grandiosity (in publishing the miracles and building the basilica), a grandeur that he felt some of the brothers wished to take upon themselves.[57]

This period of Giles's life, as already noted, coincided with the production of numerous Franciscan hagiographical documents.[58] In 1260, for instance, Bonaventure consulted him when writing his *Legenda Major*.[59] He questioned Giles not only on Francis, but on his own visionary experiences and demonic tribulations at Cetona. Giles by then was considered an authority on contemplative life, and his reputation as a mystic had grown over the years. In his *Legenda Major*, Bonaventure was to observe that he himself was an eyewitness that Giles was so often rapt into God in ecstasy that "he seemed to live among people more like an angel than a human being."[60] Bonaventure adopted Giles's teaching on the stages of mystical development, as noted previously.

More on Giles's relationship with Bonaventure is also recorded. *The Chronicle of the Twenty-Four Generals* reports an oft-quoted scene. In it, Giles confronts Bonaventure and asks him, "Can a simple person love God as much as a learned one?" To which Bonaventure responds, "An old woman can do so even more than a master in theology." The text goes on, "Then Brother Giles arose in fervor of spirit and went into the garden near the part which looked toward the city and cried out and said to a woman passing by: 'Little old woman, poor and simple and unlearned, love the Lord God and you will be greater than Brother Bonaventure.'"[61] Giles's reputation as an ecstatic also involves a humorous side. We are told that young urchins of Perugia enjoyed making fun of the way he would sometimes freeze in his tracks by yelling, "Paradiso! Paradiso!" whenever they saw him.[62]

The Final Years

By 1261, Giles's strength was failing. As the day of his death drew near, he came to be assailed even more than usual by attacks from the devil. At times he was so stricken that he was unable to straighten himself while at prayer until he was freed by being sprinkled with holy water. On one occasion, apparently, the devil picked him up and locked him into such a confined space that he could not move. His muffled cries reached Brother Gratian, one of his companions, who had to summon all his strength to open the door of his cell and then had to struggle mightily to lift him to his feet.[63] On another occasion, Giles was so gripped with fear by an attack from the devil that he began to scream. This woke up the same Brother Gratian, who came to reassure him. After the meal that evening, when he was preparing to return to his cell, he said, "I await my martyrdom."[64]

Divine consolations, nonetheless, continued to accompany him. On another occasion, returning from his cell, he was filled with such great joy that he said to one of his companions "that he had found a great treasure, one so bright and so splendid that he could not find words to describe it." His companion who saw him said that "he seemed as if drunk with the Holy Spirit."[65] And when a brother mentioned to him that St. Francis had said that a servant of God ought always to desire to die, and to die a martyr's death, Giles replied, "For myself, I do not wish to die a better death than to die of contemplation."[66]

Giles died at Monteripido on April 23, 1262. The brothers buried him in an ancient marble sarcophagus, on whose side was carved the story of Jonah.[67] Healing miracles were attributed to him while he was still alive but none after his death—a grace he had asked for from God.[68] The documents are silent on his miracles, no doubt because of his influence on the Spirituals and his personal opposition to miracles. A hundred years would go by before twenty miracles would be attributed to him in the *De Conformitate* of Bartholomew of Pisa.[69] In 1439, Perugia honored his remains. Pope Pius VI beatified him in 1777. His relics are preserved in the oratory of San Bernardino, which is located near the city gates of Perugia. Claims for his holiness are not based primarily on his healing gifts, but on the memory of his exemplary life, his tenacious fidelity to the primitive ideal, and his contemplative gifts.[70]

Giles, the third member of the founding fraternity, incarnates the Franciscan ideal without compromise. His life, what we know of it, represents the lifestyle of the primitive fraternity, and his *Dicta* serve to continue the transmission of the founding intuition. They both keep alive the memory of the elders of the Order.[71] In Giles, Francis's Christian proposal of gospel life leads to its ultimate fulfillment in mystical enlightenment.[72] To be sure, much will always remain unknown and perhaps this is fitting. Yet we know that Giles's lifelong wish was to "die of contemplation."[73] His legacy is largely untapped, but his wisdom and his *Dicta* have perennial value. They speak of the here and now of the gospel journey.

> O Lady Quail, I wish to come to you in order to listen closely and hear tell of the praises of the Lord. I want to remember that you do not say "la la" [there, there], but "qua qua" [here, here], as if to say "it is not there in some other life, but here, here that you must strive to do meritorious deeds."[74]

The *Dicta* or Golden Words

For editorial purposes, we have decided to publish most of the *Dicta* of Brother Giles, omitting the *Prologue* and chapters 11, 16, 17, 18, 20, 21, 23, 25, and 26. Certain themes found in these chapters were developed more extensively in the rest of the corpus of the *Dicta*; other themes seemed less relevant for the presentation of Giles's legacy. We have published the remaining *Dicta* because of their importance and their influence on medieval piety. We have abridged several sayings because some were recurrent or had been quoted previously as material for his biography. Ellipses indicate omitted material. The result remains an impressive treasure of spiritual wisdom and testimony of a genuine mystic.

Prologue [omitted][75]

Chapter 1. On Virtues and Graces and Their Effects and Conversely on Vices

...Purity of the heart sees God; devotion devours God.... Blessed is the one who loves and does not desire, as a result, to be loved. Blessed is the one who fears and does not desire to be feared. Blessed is the one who serves and does not desire to be served. Blessed is the one who treats others well and does not desire to be treated well by others. And because these are great matters, the foolish do not attain them.

There are three very great and useful matters, and whoever has them cannot fall into evil. The first is if you bear in peace, for God's sake, every tribulation that may befall you. The second is if you are made more humble by everything you do and receive. The third is if you love faithfully those good things that cannot be seen with your bodily eyes.[76]

Chapter 2. On Faith and the Incomprehensibility of God

Everything conceivable, everything that can be seen, told, and felt, is nothing compared to those things that cannot be conceived of, told of, seen, or felt.

All the wise and holy ones who were, who are, and who will be, who have spoken or will speak about God, have not said and never will say anything at all about God, compared to what God is, except like a little pinprick compared to heaven and earth and all creatures in them, and more than a thousand times less even than that. For all of Sacred Scripture talks to us as if in baby talk, the way a mother talks baby talk with her little child, because otherwise the child could not understand her words.

Brother Giles said to a certain secular judge, "Do you believe that God's gifts are great?" "I do," answered the judge. Brother Giles said to him, "I will show you that you don't believe it," and added, "How much are all your possessions worth?" The judge said, "Maybe a thousand libras." Brother Giles said to him, "Would you part with them for ten thousand libras?" "I would most gladly." Brother Giles said to him, "Surely, all earthly things are nothing compared to the heavenly; so why do you not give up the one for the other?" The judge answered, "Do you believe that anyone does exactly what they believe?" Brother Giles answered, "Good holy men and women have made an effort to put into practice the good things they believed, and worked at what they could do; and what they were not able to accomplish in deeds, they accomplished in holy desires: holy desire has made up for what is lacking in deeds. If anyone were to have perfect faith, they would come into such a state where full certitude would be given them. So, if you believe well, you will do well."...

A sinner, nonetheless, should never despair of receiving God's mercy as long as he or she lives. There is hardly any tree that has so many knots and thorns that it could not be planed, made beautiful, and ornate. Even more so, there is no sinner in the world so full of serious sin whom God could not in many ways adorn with grace and virtues.[77]

Chapter 3. On Love

...Whatever is without charity and love is not pleasing to God and God's saints.

You become poor through your own works and rich through divine works. So you should love the works of God and despise your own.

What is greater than to know how to praise the gifts of God and to reproach oneself for one's bad actions? I would wish to have studied in that school from the beginning of time, and to study in it until the end of time, if I had lived so long, or would be going to live so long: that is, in considering and praising the gifts of God and considering and reproaching myself for my wrongdoings. And even if I were defective in reproaching myself for my wrongdoings, I would not want to be defective in acknowledging the gifts of God.

You see how mimes and minstrels lavish praise on those who give them a little piece of clothing; what, then, should we do for the Lord our God!

You ought to be very faithful in the love of the one who wishes to free you from all that is evil and who wishes to give you all that is good.[78]

Chapter 4. On Holy Humility

No one can attain knowledge of God except through humility. The way up is to go down.

All the dangers and great downfalls that have taken place in the world would never have happened without someone holding their head high, as can be seen in the angel who was created in heaven [Lucifer], in Adam, the Pharisee in the Gospel, and many others. And all the great good things that have happened, have been done by the bowing of one's head, as can be seen in the Blessed Virgin, the publican, the good thief, and many others.

Brother Giles also said, "If only we could have a heavy weight that would always make us bow our head!"

One of the brothers said to him, "How can we flee from this pride?" And he said, "Wash your hands of it and put your mouth where you have your feet. If you consider the gifts of God, you should bow your head, and, if you consider your sins, you should likewise bow your head. Woe, however, to those who want to be honored for their wickedness!"...

Humility does not know how to speak, and patience does not dare to speak.

Humility seems to me like lightning; for as lightning strikes terrible blows, and afterward there is nothing left of what was there, humility, likewise, dissolves all evil and is the enemy of all sin and makes a person consider oneself to be nothing.[79]

Chapter 5. On the Holy Fear of the Lord

The holy fear of the Lord expels every bad fear and protects those things that cannot be expressed or even imagined. It is not given to all to have this fear, for it is a very great gift.

Those who do not fear show that they have nothing to lose.

The fear of the Lord is what rules and governs men and women and leads them into the Lord's grace. If one has that grace, the fear of the Lord preserves it, and if one does not have it, the fear of the Lord leads to it. All the rational creatures that have fallen would never have fallen if they had had this gift. This holy gift is given only to holy men and women. And inasmuch as some are more graced, they are no less humble and God fearing. And this less-practiced virtue is not less than the others....

Be always fearful and wary of yourself and of anyone like yourself....

This fear makes us obey humbly and bow our head all the way down to the ground under the yoke of holy obedience.

Also, the more fear we have, the more we pray. And it is no small thing to be given the grace of holy prayer.

No matter how great they seem to be, human works are not as they are in the estimation of human beings, but are as God esteems them and is pleased by them. And so it is good for us to have holy fear at all times.[80]

Chapter 6. On Patience

…To the extent that someone is ready to bear tribulations and insults for God's sake, that is how great they are in God's sight, and no more. And the weaker one is in enduring tribulations and suffering for God, the less one is in God's sight; and such a person does not really know what God is.…

We are not good at bearing tribulations, because we are not good at pursuing spiritual consolations. In fact, the one who faithfully works in, and on, and for oneself would find all things sweet to bear.…

To bear tribulations without complaining purges sins more than a flow of tears.…

One of the brothers said to him, "What shall we do if great tribulations occur in our time?" Brother Giles responded, "If the Lord rained down stones and rocks from heaven, they would not hurt us if we were what we should be. If someone is what they are meant to be, evil would be changed into good for them. For just as good itself is changed into evil for a person of ill will, so evil is changed into good for a person of good will. For, in fact, all great things, good and bad, lie within people, where they cannot be seen."…

Once, one of the brothers was grumbling in his presence about some heavy task of obedience that had been laid on him. The holy brother Giles said to him, "My friend, the more you grumble, the more you burden yourself. And the more devoutly and humbly you bow your head under the yoke of holy obedience, the lighter and pleasanter it will be for you. You do not want to be disparaged in this world and yet you want to be honored in the other? You do not want to be cursed and yet you want to be blessed? You do not want to labor and yet you want to find rest? You are deceived, for it is through disparagement that you come to honor, through being cursed that you obtain blessings, and through labor, rest. The proverb is true: 'The one who does not give what he is sorry to lose cannot have what he desires.' Don't be surprised if your neighbor offends you sometimes, because even Martha, who was holy, wished to provoke the Lord against her own sister. But Martha's complaint against Mary was unjust, because the more Mary lost the use of her body, compared to Martha (for Mary had lost her speech, sight, hearing, taste, and movement), so much more work she did than Martha.[81] Strive to be grace filled and virtuous, and fight against vices, and bear tribulations and shame with patience. For there is nothing else, if you do not conquer yourself, because it counts for little if one draws souls to God, without conquering oneself."[82]

Chapter 7. On Holy Solicitude and a Vigilant Heart

…If you can be safe, don't put yourself at risk. The one who works for God and for the everlasting kingdom is safe.…

Just as an evil idleness is a way to go to hell, so a holy idleness and quiet are a way to go to heaven.

One should be very solicitous to guard well the grace God gives and to work faithfully with it. For often one loses the fruit for sake of the leaves and the grain for sake of the chaff.…

What a lot of water the river Tiber would hold if it were not continually flowing out!…

Once holy brother Giles said to someone who wished to go to Rome, "When you are on your way, do not take to yourself any of the things you see, lest they become a hindrance to you. Know how to tell genuine money from counterfeit. For the enemy is very clever and he has many hidden traps."…

If all the fields and the vineyards in the world belonged to one man and he did not cultivate them or have them cultivated, what produce would he get from them? While another man who had a small number of fields and vineyards and cultivated them well would get produce from them for himself and for many others.…

Unless one prepares a place within oneself for God, one will never find a place among the creatures of God.…

Then one of the brothers said to him, "Perhaps we will die before we know our own good and before we experience anything good." Brother Giles answered, "Tanners know about hides, shoemakers about shoes, smiths about iron, and so on in other crafts. But how can a person know a craft they have never worked at? Do you think that great lords give great gifts to stupid and crazy people? They do not."[83]

Chapter 8. On Contempt for the World

Woe to the one who puts one's heart, desire, and energy into the things of this world and on their account gives up and loses the things that are of heaven and last forever!

The high-flying eagle would not fly so high if it had one of the beams of St. Peter's tied to either of its wings.

I find many people who work for the needs of their body and few who work for their soul. For many work for their body by breaking rocks, making tunnels in mountains, and other such difficult jobs. But who works so energetically and fervently for the needs of their soul?

The greedy person is like a mole that does not believe there is any treasure or any other good but to tunnel in the ground and live there. Yet there are many other treasures that it is unaware of.

The birds of the air and the beasts of the earth and the fishes of the sea are satisfied when they have their proper food. So, since people are not satisfied with the things of this world, but are always longing for something else, it is clear that they were not made primarily for these things but for others. For the body was made for the soul, and this world for the sake of the other world.[84]

Chapter 9. On Holy Chastity

Our flesh is like a hog that runs eagerly into the mud hole and enjoys wallowing there.

The flesh is like a dung beetle that enjoys poking about in horse manure....

Our flesh is the devil's plantation.

A man who has an animal on loan gets as much use out of it as he can. That is what we ought to do with the body....

One of the brothers said to him, "How can we avoid the vices of the flesh?" Holy brother Giles answered him, "The one who wants to move big rocks and large beams tries to move them more by cleverness than by strength. And in this matter we must proceed the same way."

Every vice wounds chastity. Chastity is like a clear mirror that can be clouded just by breathing on it.

It is impossible to come to the grace of God as long as you like to enjoy sensual things. So you can turn this way and that, up and down, to one side and the other, but there is no other way than to fight against the flesh that wants to betray you day and night. The one who overcomes it overcomes all enemies and attains all that is good....

One of the brothers said to him, "Isn't charity a greater virtue than chastity?" Holy brother Giles answered him, "And what is more chaste than charity?"...

After this, he said, "Look, O human, at what you love and to what end you love it: heaven or earth, the Creator or the creature, light or darkness, the flesh or the spirit, good or evil. Then you will be better able to separate the good from the bad and see what you ought to love and what you ought to hate."[85]

Chapter 10. On the Fight against Temptations

...Someone told him, "I am often tempted horribly and many times I have asked the Lord to take this from me, but he does not." Holy brother Giles answered him, "The better the armor a king gives his soldiers, the more fiercely he wants them to join in the battle."

And then one of the brothers asked him, "How can I go eagerly to prayer when I feel dry and without enthusiasm?" He answered, "Listen. A king has two servants, one of whom is armed and the other unarmed; they both must go to war. The armed one goes bravely to war while the unarmed servant says to his lord, 'My lord, as you see, I have no weapons; but because I love you, I will go forth into battle even without weapons.' When the king sees the faithfulness of this servant, he says to his officers, 'Go and prepare weapons for this faithful servant of mine, and place on him the sign of my own armor." And if someone goes into the battle of prayer unarmed, as it were, because they feel dry and lacking in devotion, God sees their faithfulness and places on them the very sign of his own armor."...

On another occasion someone told him, "What can I do? If I do something good, I get vain about it. And if I do something bad, I get sad and almost despair." Holy brother Giles answered, "You do well to feel sorrow for your sin. However, I advise you to feel sad with moderation; you must always believe that God's power to pardon is greater than your power to sin. And if God grants mercy to any great sinner, do you believe he will abandon a small sinner? Also, do not stop doing good because your are tempted by vainglory. If a farmer, about to sow seed in the ground, said to himself, 'I don't want to sow this year because birds may come and eat my grain,' and because of that, he didn't sow, he would have no produce from his land to eat. But if he sows, although he might lose a little, still the greater part would be his. That is the way it is with the one who is tempted by vainglory but fights it."[86]

Chapter 11. On Penance [omitted][87]

Chapter 12. On Prayer and Its Effects

Prayer is the beginning and the completion of all good....

The one who does not know how to pray does not know God....

One of the brothers told him, "A person should find it very painful when they cannot find in prayer the grace of devotion." Brother Giles responded, "I advise you to go slow on this matter. For if you knew there was some good wine in a cask and there was a sediment at the bottom, would you shake the cask and mix the wine with the sediment? That would not be the thing to do. And if the grindstone of a mill sometimes does not make good flour, the miller does not immediately smash it with a hammer, but he repairs the grindstone slowly and gradually, and then it makes good flour. Do likewise, and consider that you, in no way, deserve to receive any consolation from God in prayer. For if someone had lived from the beginning of the world until now and were to live on until the end of the world, and they wept a bowl full of tears every day in prayer, even then, they would not be worthy at the end of the world that God should grant them one single consolation.".…

Someone said to him, "I see many who seem to experience the grace of devotion and tears immediately when they pray. But I can hardly feel anything as a result of prayer." Brother Giles responded, "Labor faithfully and devoutly because the grace that God does not give you at one time, he may give at another time, and what God does not give you on one day or one week, or month or year, he could give you another day or another week or month or year. Place your labor humbly in God and God will place his grace in you as it pleases him. A metal worker making a knife strikes many blows on the iron out of which he is making the knife, even before the knife is finished; but, finally, the knife is finished with one blow.".…

He also said, "Many good deeds are commended in the Holy Scripture: to clothe the naked, feed the hungry, and many others. However, speaking about prayer, the Lord says, 'The Father seeks such people to worship him.' Good deeds adorn the soul, but prayer is something great beyond measure."

Holy religious are like wolves who hardly ever go out in public except for some great necessity, and then they don't stay there long.…

He also said this about himself: "I would rather be blind than be the handsomest or the richest or the wisest or the noblest person in the world." Someone said to him, "Why would you rather be blind than to have all those things?" "Because," he replied, "I am afraid they would hinder me on my journey."[88]

Chapter 13. On Contemplation

One time, brother Giles asked one of the brothers, "What do your wise men say contemplation is?" And he said, "I don't know." "Do you want me to tell you what it seems to me to be?" "I do." And holy brother Giles said, "There are seven levels of contemplation: fire, anointing, ecstasy, contemplation, taste, rest, and glory."

"I say *fire*: that is, the light that precedes the enlightenment of the soul. Then, *anointing* with ointments, from which there rises a marvelous fragrance, which follows that light; as it says in the Song of Songs, *In the fragrance of your ointments*, and so on. After this, *ecstasy*, for when the fragrance is experienced, the soul is snatched up and taken away from the senses of the body. Then *contemplation* follows, for after the soul is drawn away from the bodily senses, it contemplates God in a marvelous way. After this comes *taste*, for in contemplation the soul experiences a wondrous sweetness, about which the Psalm speaks: *Taste and see*, and so on. Next *rest*, for when the spiritual palate has been sweetened, the soul rests in that sweetness. Finally, *glory* follows, for the soul glories in such rest and is refreshed with tremendous joy; whence the Psalm says, *I will have everything I could want, when your glory appears."*

He also said, "No one is able to rise to the contemplation of the glory of the divine majesty except by fervor of spirit and frequent prayer. One is enflamed by fervor of spirit and rises to contemplation when the heart, along with the other members, is fully disposed for this in such a way that it wants nothing else, can think of nothing else, than what it has and is experiencing."

To live the contemplative life is to leave behind all earthly things for the love of God, to seek only the things of heaven, to pray assiduously, to read often and avidly, to constantly praise God with hymns and canticles.

To contemplate is to be cut off from all things and to be joined only to God.

Again he said, "The good contemplator is somebody who, if they had their hands and feet cut off, and their eyes put out, and their nose, ears, and tongue cut off, wouldn't care; because of the immensity of the most sweet, ineffable, and inestimable fragrance, joy, and pleasantness, they wouldn't care about, or want to have, any other members, or anything else imaginable concerning heaven, than what they have and are experiencing: just as Mary, sitting at the feet of the Lord received such pleasure from the words of God that no part of her was able to do or to want to do anything but what it was doing. As shown by the fact that when her sister complained that she wasn't helping her, she didn't answer by any word or gesture; Christ became her spokesman, answering for Mary, who could not answer for herself."[89]

Chapter 14. On the Active Life

Since no one would be able to successfully undertake the contemplative life without first having undergone faithful and dedicated training in the active life, one ought to work hard and diligently in the practice of the active life.

A good practitioner of the active life would be someone who, if it were possible, would feed all the poor people of this world, clothe them all, give them an abundance of everything they need, and build all the churches and hostels and bridges of this world. Then, after all this, if everyone in the world considered them to be bad, and they were well aware of it, they would not want to be considered anything but bad, and would not stop doing any good work on account of this, but would apply themselves with greater fervor to every good work, like one who neither wishes nor desires nor expects any credit in this world as recompense. Just as Martha, solicitous about constant serving, when she asked to be helped by her sister, was rebuked by the Lord and yet did not stop her good work; so also the good active worker ought not to stop doing good work because of any rebuke or contempt, because they do not expect an earthly reward for this, but an eternal one.

Again he said, "If you find grace in prayer, pray; and if you don't find it, pray; because God accepted even goat hair as an offering."

Sometimes, the king has more love for the foot of someone who does less work for him, than he loves the whole person of someone else who does more work for him, for *the Lord sees the heart*.[90]

Chapter 15. On the Ongoing Practice of Spiritual Caution

If you want to see well, tear out your eyes and be blind. If you want to hear well, be deaf. If you want to walk well, cut off your feet. If you want to work well, cut off your hands. If you want to love well, hate yourself. If you want to live well, die to yourself. If you want to make a good profit, know how to lose. If you want to be rich, be poor. If you want pleasure, make yourself miserable. If you want to be secure, always be afraid. If you want to be exalted, humble your-self. If you want to be honored, despise yourself and honor those who despise you. If you want to have good, endure evil. If you want to rest, then work. If you want to be blessed, desire to be cursed. Oh, what great wisdom it is to know how to do this! But because these are great things, they are not given to all....

People imagine God the way they want God to be, but God is always just the way God is.[91]

Chapter 16. On Useful and Useless Knowledge and on the Preachers of the Word of God [omitted][92]

Chapter 17. On Good and Bad Speech [omitted][93]

Chapter 18. On Persevering in Doing Good [omitted][94]

Chapter 19. On Religious Life and Its Security

Speaking of himself, brother Giles used to say, "I would rather enjoy a few graces from God in religious life than many while living in the world, because there are more dangers and fewer aids in the world than in religious life. But sinners fear what is for their own good more than they fear their own evil. They fear more the thought of doing penance and entering religious life than remaining in sin in a worldly life."...

He also said, "It seems to me that the Order of Friars Minor truly was sent into this world for the great benefit of men and women; but woe to us if we are not what we should be! The Order of Friars Minor seems to me the poorest and the richest in this world. But this seems to me our greatest fault: we want to walk with those who are too high up. They are rich who make themselves resemble the rich; they are wise who make themselves resemble the wise; they are good who make themselves resemble the good; they are beauti-ful who make themselves resemble the beautiful; they are noble who make themselves resemble the noble—namely, Our Lord Jesus Christ."[95]

Chapter 20. On the Usefulness of Obedience [omitted][96]

Chapter 21. On Remembering Death [omitted][97]

Chapter 22. On Flight from the World

Good company is like an antidote; bad company is like venom.

Trees next to the road and the traffic of the road are sometimes chopped away at by passersby, so they are prevented from bearing their fruit to maturity. In the same way, it harms one to stay out in public.[98]

Chapter 23. On Persevering in Prayer [omitted][99]

Chapter 24. On the Graces and Virtues Obtained in Prayer

Many are the graces and virtues to be encountered and acquired in prayer. First, one's mind is enlightened; second, one's faith is strengthened; third, one comes to know one's own miserable condition; fourth, one arrives at holy fear, and is humbled and has a low opinion of oneself; fifth, one achieves a contrite heart; sixth, one's conscience is purified; seventh, one is made steady in patience; eighth, one submits to obedience; ninth, one arrives at true discernment; tenth, one arrives at knowledge; eleventh, at understanding; twelfth, at fortitude; thirteenth, at wisdom; fourteenth, at knowledge of God, who makes himself known to those "who worship him in spirit and in truth." After one is set on fire in love, one runs in the fragrance [of holy anointing], arrives at the experience of tender sweetness, is led into rest for the mind, and finally, is conducted into glory. But once a person has put their mouth to the words of God, where one's soul is satisfied, who could ever be able to tear such a one away from prayer, which has led to such contemplation? As St. Gregory says, "Once the heavenly sweetness has been tasted, all things found on earth become worthless."

But for one to arrive at the state just mentioned, six things are necessary, among many others: first, the consideration of one's past evil deeds, for which one ought to feel sorrow; second, caution concerning present evil; third, fear of future evil; fourth, a consideration of the mercy of God, who is waiting for each person, not doing judgment because of their sins, although anyone in mortal sin would deserve eternal punishment according to divine justice; fifth, a consideration of God's good gifts, which can never be adequately expounded—that is, the flesh that he assumed for us, the suffering that he endured for us, and the teaching that he left for us; and sixth, consideration of the glory that he has promised us.[100]

Chapter 25. On Prelates' Negligence in the Matter of the Canonization of Certain Brothers [omitted][101]

Chapter 26. How Blessed Giles Explained a Few Important Questions [omitted][102]

II

ROGER OF PROVENCE

Between Agony and Ecstasy

Introduction

Raymond Petri is the main source for whatever we know about Roger of Provence. He reports that Roger's ecstatic preaching was so powerful that once he became inflamed with fervor, he was unable to stop. He preached one Sunday afternoon and during the entire meal in the community refectory. After the meal, he kept with him three friars, Raymond among them, and still in a frenzied state, went on preaching for almost half the night. Raymond reports that "looking up to heaven," Roger spoke, "as if reading from a book, such deep and profound mysteries unheard of by the world that no one could really remember them or understand them." His words, nonetheless, reverberated with tremendous impact. After listening to them for some two hours, one of the friars felt that his chest was going to split open. In fear of dying, he got Roger to stop talking by shouting three times that Matins was about to begin. By transfer mechanism, the fervor of what was transmitted through Roger's ecstatic preaching led to the near-death experience of his petrified auditor. As for Roger, he did extreme violence to himself and managed to stop speaking. When he came back to his senses, he too was stupefied by what had taken place. "What could the brothers be thinking, he said, if they heard such words? They would say I was speaking Greek."[1]

A quick glimpse at Roger's biography will set the tone for the presentation of his *Meditations*.

THE EARLIEST FRANCISCANS

Biography

The biography of this famous Franciscan comes from two sources: *The Chronicle of the Twenty-Four Generals*, written in large part before 1366 and completed in 1374 by Arnold of Sarrant, and a fifteenth-century manuscript preserved by the Bollandists of a much older work on which the accounts in the *Chronicle* depend. The author of the narratives contained in both sources is Brother Raymond, Roger's confessor. He assembles his data as he pleases, in the form of testimonies that he culled from his frequent exchanges with Roger, whom he refers to as his *custos*, therefore his prelate, and at times, *pater*.[2] The reader is confronted with a collection of confidences rather than an official *Vita*; there are no dates and no information prior to his conversion. Many testimonies begin with *sicut ipse dicebat* (as he himself said), referring to the confidences between the two men. In the *Chronicle*, Roger's *Vita* and *Meditations* are situated right after the mention of Brother Athloti of Prato, who was the eleventh Minister General of the Order from 1285 to 1286. Raymond's testimony then follows with the opening expression *vivebat tunc*, suggesting that Roger lived at that time.[3]

The Conversion of a Learned Man

We know little of Roger before his entry into the Franciscan Order around 1297. By then, he had already received a clerical and theological formation. This explains why, three years after his entry, he could be named master of novices for some twenty friars in Montpellier and, in 1301, *custos* (regional superior) in Avignon, a position that he held until his death. The twelve years he lived as a Franciscan included sojourns in Tarascon and Narbonne.[4] Probably it was during these years that he wrote his *Meditations*. We know that he studied and meditated on the Holy Scriptures on a daily basis, relying on the commentaries and interpretations of the Pseudo-Dionysius, Saint Augustine, and Hugh of Saint Victor.[5]

Roger's conversion is the point of departure for his spiritual life. What triggered it is unknown, but whatever its nature, it left profound traces in his psyche and became emblematic of the inner turmoil of his entire journey. He describes it as "a total mutation," one so radical that "it could only be attributed to an intervention from the right hand of the Most High." This turning point was followed by such a terrible temptation, that horrified and trembling at the thought of it, he repeated three times, "In the presence of God there could not ever be a greater temptation." He was able to overcome his temptation, inundated with such extraordinary graces that henceforth he could not sin mortally. Roger never went into details about it. Raymond deduced that the temptation was one of despair in view of the enormity of his sins and his longing for forgiveness. Roger's interpretation of the event is reported as follows: "Once I had experienced such sorrow over my sins that after this sorrow I knew—and the source of my knowledge is an absolutely sure one—that God forgave me and spared me the guilt and the culpability due to all my sins."[6]

Throughout his life, the man was assailed with scrupulosity, confessing himself as many as twenty times a day, not only to Raymond, but to all the friars of the convent, not to mention five or six general confessions each year, needing at times months to recover. He would come back to the same fault, even the least one, not only over the course of many confessions, but even in the same one, detecting nuances hardly distinct from one another.[7] Such compulsive behavior indicates the intersection of the pathological and the mystical; his preaching also emphatically demonstrates his taste for the excessive. A close reading of Roger's *Vita* reveals that his frequent anxiety attacks often put him on the fringe of community life.[8]

A Man of Extremes

A simple invitation to prayer, like *Deus in adjutorium*, would force Roger out of reality and throw him into a state of raging frenzy, whether in the garden or in the chapel for Divine Office. The friars often saw him roam around hysterically, crying or shouting his head off; at other times, they witnessed his trances like a mad man. He never looked at a woman for three years, not even his aging mother, a saintly person; women terrified him. He ran away at the very thought that one would want to speak to him.

Roger multiplied fasting practices and disciplined his body mercilessly. Before each blow to the body, he raised his spirit to heaven in prayer. Roger adopted this practice of elevating his mind to God, often in the form of mantras,[9] before many of his actions, even the most ordinary ones. During meals, for instance, he would precede every bite of food by prayer "so as not to taste," as he put it, "the savor of the food." And if he did not succeed in this elevation, he simply did not eat. This practice also preceded each response of the Divine Office, which he recited with his confessor. Roger's elevation of the mind to God served to maintain strict guard over his senses and sustain his desire for God; and it triggered states of illumination with bizarre outer manifestations.[10] At the core of such extreme behavior, and his elevating his mind in God, lies a fearful obsession with sin.[11]

Repeated Ecstasies

Many of Roger's ecstasies took place while celebrating daily Mass, which often took three to four hours. He celebrated with such frenzied movements that some thought he would lose his balance and fall flat on the ground. Some friars were afraid to serve his Mass for this reason. As for Roger, commenting on his style of presiding, he told Raymond, speaking of himself in the third person, "This man when he celebrates the Mass does not know what he is doing; all his gestures and words take place through an intermediary, for when they take place, his soul is completely united to God."[12] Once after Mass, while taking off his vestments, he was seen breathing heavily, grinding his teeth, trembling uncontrollably, his hands rigid, speechless, and running off without folding his vestments. According to Raymond, "Many thought he was insane." During another celebration, he became so raptured and lifted to such heights that it seemed to him that "he was God."[13] The experience in itself was so unbearable, Raymond recalls Roger as saying, "Lord, leave me, for I cannot stand the abundance of your sweetness." This experience was communicated with great fear, and his confessor was ordered never to speak about it to anyone.

A powerful ecstatic episode took place in the final year of his life during Holy Week. It illustrates the excessive states into which he fell so often. Roger once wandered about the garden in the friary for three days crying out, "When will I die, oh Lord, when will I die?" Raymond went to him to find out what was going on and recalls,

"Roger met me like a man who was drunk, with his entire face so red and enflamed that it was as if fire emanated from it and his eyes glared eerily like a madman. His demeanor was so terrifying, that I did not dare to speak to him or to look at him."

Roger could only say, "Who can bear that so much fire can burn in such vile matter? Who can bear that the soul dwells so close to God in such miserable estate? Why should someone live if one has attained such a state that with every movement of the heart one turns to God, sees nothing but God, thinks about nothing except God, desires nor feels nothing other than Him?"[14]

Roger could slip into ecstatic states with great ease. Speaking of himself again in the third person, he confessed how easy it was to be enraptured: "I know of a man who experienced raptures up to a hundred times during the recitation of one Matins at almost every verse."[15] Some friars even witnessed a fiery globe surrounding him, while he stood immobile as if asleep, his face covered by his capuche. He confessed that he had to use strength to flee God in such instances as others try to come near him; the very fact of fixing his eyes even for a moment on God caused in him the fear of never returning from that state. His numerous accounts reveal a constant paradox: Roger would experience the sweetness of God as something violent and uncontrollable, out of touch with reality; and yet he was able to adorn his accounts with images, visions of angels and saints, or even vigorous dialogues between himself and his soul, or himself and God.[16] Several *Meditations* result from his ecstatic episodes.

A Death Unnoticed

Roger's twelve years as a Franciscan in Provence ended unnoticed. He died in Uzès around 1309 or 1310, leaving no legacy of popular devotion and no reputation as a healer to his account. The only miracle mentioned in his *Vita* concerns a very sick woman walking effortlessly to his tomb as if her feet did not touch the ground.[17] His death resembles his short existence as a friar; he lived cut off from public life because of his excessive behavior. Till the end, he is remembered as a "venerable" man eager to die because life seemed so intolerable to him. The impact he had on his Franciscan brothers was due more to his teachings than his ecstatic episodes. Yet one must acknowledge that the richness of his ecstasies became a way of preaching, even if marked by agony and torment. The difference between authentic mystical experience and pathological behavior may never be clarified; but the connection between the two showed enough fruit for Roger to serve as master to his brothers and produce his *Meditations*.

Roger's Franciscan Lineage

Roger reveals himself to be a true descendant of such mystics as Francis and Giles of Assisi, Conrad of Offida, and John of La Verna, who were all credited with visionary experiences. Francis rarely spoke of his personal experiences; yet his biographers often report his many ecstatic episodes climaxed by the reception of the stigmata on Mount La Verna.[18] Giles became a figure of authority for Roger because of his ecstatic reputation and his degrees of contemplation.[19] A close kinship tied these men of God together: they felt very strongly that their visions were not to be disclosed. Any account would have been like betraying them or altering the truth.

Roger also shares a spiritual lineage with the Franciscan Spirituals Hugh of Digne, his sister Douceline, Peter Olivi, and Na Prous Boneta, although none of them are mentioned in Roger's *Vita* or in his *Meditations*. Unlike the Franciscan Spirituals, he never mentions Francis's *Rule* and *Testament*, nor does he allude to the foundational elements such as fraternity, work, begging, and relationship to money. There is no mention whatsoever of poverty or the poverty debate so alive in the circles he is moving in. Roger makes no use of the Joachimite apocalyptic speculation so prominent among his Provençal contemporaries or even the Passion-centered mysticism of much of the writings of the Spirituals. Yet he is part of the dissident Franciscan wing because of his insistence on the *kenosis* of Christ crucified and the "necessity of bearing in one's body the stigmata of Jesus Christ" as the true sign of life. Finally, the radical quest for contemplation and the importance of the Eucharist appear as other trademarks relating him to the Spirituals.

Presentation of the *Meditations*

The corpus of forty *Meditations* is found in the *Chronicle of the Twenty-Four Generals*, like a series of reflections, one after the other, in language at times obscure and ungrammatical.[20] One could also label them personal considerations or exhortations because of their opening verbs, *considera* and *attende*. The entire work indicates a spiritual maturity attained over the years and has echos of Roger's visionary encounters with God and Christ. It also fits in the same lineage as the *Apophthegma* of the Desert Fathers, the *Admonitions* of Francis, the *Golden Words* of Brother Giles, and the sayings of Jacopone da Todi. The ensemble is addressed mostly to the friars.[21] Each text is brief, standing by itself on a particular theme, and presses the reader to attend to one's life in God.

It is impossible to date the first publication of the *Meditations*. One can theorize that the corpus of *Meditations* began circulating between 1310, the date of Roger's death, and 1332, the date of the appearance of the Avignon manuscript, which refers to it explicitly, thus indicating the diffusion of the *Meditations*.[22] The official appearance of the text in the *Chronicle*, in its final form, has scholars thinking that his teaching was accessible to Franciscan circles during the first half of the fifteenth century. Like the writings of Francis and Giles, the *Meditations* started out orally, through Roger's teachings; they were then culled one after the other in the form of *reportationes*, and finally, assembled in a corpus to be published after some twenty years.

The *Meditations* express a recurrent theme found in the Book of Exodus in the Bible: God is the one who is and before whom all other created reality is as nonbeing.[23] The vocabulary used and the spirituality emerging from the text show a strong Pseudo-Dionysian influence. Roger is associated with the current of essence mysticism widespread at the time, especially among the Beguines. One associates Roger with the same apophatic current as Angela of Foligno, Jacopone of Todi, Guibert of Tournai, Hadewijch of Anvers, Marguerite Porete, and Master Eckhart. Like them, Roger insists on the inexpressibility of God: no one can speak fittingly about him.

Even though more than seventy years set Francis and Roger apart, there is a common ground between them when they evoke the unchangeableness and the ineffability of God.[24] Roger's *Meditations* bear the stamp of his Franciscan heritage. This is especially true in his admiration for all of created reality considered as a ladder to climb to God and as cosmic reality singing God's praises. Much like Francis, Roger insists on the need for detachment and nonappropriation of anything to oneself that is foreign to God, the importance of silence, the avoidance of meaningless conversations, the need to preserve one's sacred intimacy with God instead of disclosing it to others.[25] Roger never directly alludes to his experiences throughout the *Meditations*; he disdains the gift of tears for fear that these will attract attention to himself instead of God. He also uses the same language as Francis on the scorn and distrust of the body. It is important to keep in mind the autobiographical resonances whenever the text refers to the experience of God and God's being.[26]

The *Meditations*[27]

1. Inspired with divine exhortation we say to the just one, rejoice! As in the third chapter of Isaiah: *Say to the just that it will be well with them, for of the fruit of their works they will eat.* For the just are in communion with God through their works. Those words that Isaiah attributes to the just person, holy David speaks of as properly God's; he says, *I will meditate on all your works.* They are said to be properly divine because without the aid of the one who searches hearts, the human mind searches in vain for divine realities. But when the Spirit dwells in one's soul, the saying is shown to be most divinely said: *The Spirit searches all things, even the depths of God.* Exulting in these things, the just one will discover God, then make this discovery known to others so that they, too, might see his name exalted and always seek his face.[28]

2. Look, therefore, and see the Church's faithfulness to God, see whether she considers it wise to cling to God. *To cling to God,* she says, *is my good.* And this good is the good of all goods. Look and see what are the good things of our heavenly homeland and the miseries of this earthly exile. See what great rever-

ence you should have toward God and toward the God-Man. Because of this human who is God, you should have such high regard for every human person that you hardly dare to look anyone in the face. Look and see yourself; an altogether vile worm, an insignificant bit of dust, but a human nonetheless, and, as such, you should keep yourself clean of all sin for the sake of him who ought to be glorified in you—that is to say, God.[29]

3. Look and see the desire of the angels: they would wish all humans to be exalted higher than themselves because of the exaltation of human nature that they behold exalted above them, in God. Now if the angels, who are so great, have such a desire, what reverence ought you to have toward every human person, since each one is an image of God. Take a good look at yourself and see what reverence you ought to have for the angel, whom you have always as a guardian, who is always and everywhere present to you, and through whom also God bestows upon you countless benefits.[30]

4. Consider the words in the Psalm: *You have made known to me the paths of life.* For there are two paths: the path of divinity by which we consider the things of God, and the path of humanity by which we consider the things that are a human's in God. Therefore, take great care that you do not harbor within yourself anything that is foreign to God, for *from his fullness we have all received.* Consider well and impress this firmly within yourself: God is, and God alone is, and anything else that is made is as if it were not.[31]

5. Consider and see that you order your affections so that you are not affected by any of the things you see but rather by those you do not see. For the things you see are but a shadow or a thin vapor of those that cannot be seen. Consider this and strive to judge things accurately, so that you will take each of them at its true value. So, for instance, those that are temporal, may you judge to be temporal and as if nonexistent; but may those things that are invisible remain and enter into your heart.[32]

6. Consider and see that you regard it a great waste of time whenever you are not at liberty to pray. Consider that your one desire

among all things ought to be to have access to prayer, because once you find your rest and peace there you will never be able to be at rest anywhere else. For if you truly know this experience, whenever you are at liberty to do something else you will regard yourself imprisoned.[33]

7.   Consider that *where your treasure is, there also your heart* should be. Now, what is your treasure if not God and the things of God? Therefore, even though you are oppressed by the weight of the flesh, dead and constricted within this body, nonetheless dwell in spirit among the things of heaven, where you have a glorious treasure laid away. Consider this so that you do not plant your feet on any of the things under heaven. Consider and heed well: any time you feel some darkness, aridity, sorrow, sadness, or any other disorder by which you feel yourself to be far away from God or by which you are prevented from going freely to him, impute this to yourself and not to God. And may this remedy help you to go on to acknowledging, deploring, and lamenting your miserable exile.[34]

8.   Consider that whatever all the saints have done, whatever all the angels have done and are doing, whatever all of creation can do, is nothing in terms of what is worthy of God. So, what will you, poor wretch, be able to do all by yourself in your brief moment of time? Therefore let whatever you can do for God count as less than nothing in your eyes. Consider to what degradation you are subjected when you submit to the demands of your own body. Is not the flesh a most vile leper? So consider the cost, and whose servant you want to be. Consider and take very great care that you never are caught unarmed. Consider it and harden your heart to always be at odds with yourself. Who is to be obeyed: God or the devil? Spirit or flesh? The queen or the handmaid? Great is the cost, great the degradation, great the misery, if you serve or obey the flesh.[35]

9.   Look at your vocation, look at your state in life. If God has placed you in a more excellent state, then see to it that your life is more excellent. Or would you be an unfaithful and ungrateful servant of your Lord who has thus adopted you? Consider and see to it that whatever you see, whatever you hear, whatever you

understand and feel, you reflect back to the praise of God according to the second way, taking into account, first, the property of the things themselves; second, their spiritual meaning; third, their end, which is love; and fourth, true affection.[36]

10. Consider and see to it that you may always bear in your body the stigmata of our Lord Jesus Christ in your struggle to draw near to God. Consider that it was for this struggle that you were made. Would you want to frustrate the very end for which God has designed you? See how every creature attains its end. Would you want to be more miserable than every other thing that has been made? This struggle is your rest and your peace. When you put your effort into this kind of struggle, then you will begin to really exist.[37]

11. Consider and see how changeable you are, and how unchangeable is your God. Is not your heart sometimes enflamed, burning, and fainting away when it is lifted above itself into God? And is God, then, changeable? Far from it, for God is not changed in relation to you, but rather you are changed in your relation to God. When you are in such a state, then, look at where you came from, and see that God was just the same before you were with him, and so he still is, in some more than incomprehensible and ineffable way. Is God not the light that shines in the darkness? Yes, the light shines, but *the darkness did not comprehend it.* Consider that no one ever has been or is able to speak fittingly about God. Does not the power of those ineffable realities seem to be diminished as soon as human language touches them? It would certainly seem that way.[38]

12. Consider that great hope does not spring up except from something great enough to motivate it. Consider and see what motivates your desire for God, and see also how you can be consoled, by what kinds of things, or in what way. Does not desire or *hope deferred afflict the soul*? It does indeed. For if you truly desire, you experience true distress; or if you thirst for God, how could you ever be satisfied except by the taste of his spirit or by a torrent of his divine pleasures? Take heed and see to it that you are not satisfied with just any degree of virtue. Rather, with God's help, strive for what is perfect in any virtue.[39]

13. Consider and see how sweet is the lot of the angels and the blessed, and may all your striving be for this, that in everything you think and feel, you may experience something of that ineffable and unknown sweetness. For even though while on the way you can never experience it as it is, or as the angels and the blessed do, nevertheless, because you are future citizens with them, if you walk in the truth before God, he will give you, here, a foretaste of this supreme sweetness. Does not God temper by his own sweetness the bitterness of the life of those who day and night walk through the depths of the sea? How else could they survive? Is he not the God of his own? He most certainly is.[40]

14. Consider and see who is speaking where it is written, *My delight is to be with the sons of men.* If this is the delight of God, who is so great, so unthinkable, then your delight is in God, if you are in him, or insofar as you are in him by charity and in charity. When? At that point—that is to say, in that blessed inspiration—when my whole living, my whole life, will be his blessed inspiration. Because now I fall from that state and cannot yet stand firm in it. I immediately fall and lose myself in a multitude of things. I am completely scattered and my life is scattered and I cannot succeed in unifying my life. Will I ever be able to do so? Yes, I will. But when? When I live completely in God and when God alone is my whole life. Then I will be able to stand above myself and will not be compelled to return in confusion to myself. I will never again be brought low. For that place of standing firm, with no more falling away, is God.[41]

15. Consider what the just man says about pleasures: "Lord, the more I knew they were dangerous, the more bitter I regarded them; the more I knew they were opposed to the spirit, the more I refused them to the flesh; the more I realized that they were an impediment to my spirit, the more I cast them from me." Which is sweeter: To take pleasure in God or in food? The comparison is absurd. Does the one who finds pleasure in eating enjoy something created or that which is really to be enjoyed? What an aberration! It is God that is to be enjoyed. The more, therefore, that anyone is fearful of enjoying anything else except God, let them be that much more concerned with casting away all

pleasures. Pleasure derived from a creature is an obstacle to the divine sweetness, for those who pursue true pleasure in God know no pleasure in any creature. "Once one has tasted the Spirit, all flesh becomes insipid."[42]

16. Consider and see how if the Lord is present, everything becomes present to you. If in the presence of eternity; the past and the future; creation, both spirit and matter; what is being made, has been made, or will be made; knowledge, reason, and virtue; everything that has not been made, or could not possibly be made or created; what has been made; what could have been but will not be made—what ardor, eagerness, and love do you think you would feel in the face of all this? I do not doubt that you would be always taken out of yourself. This belongs to the Lord God of hosts himself alone.[43]

17. Consider and see that you take into consideration not only the things that are written, such as the kinds of knowledge handed down through human invention, but also the angels' wonderful knowledge, which you in your human state cannot achieve. And not only that wonderful knowledge of the angels, but even further, the ineffable and inscrutable source of the wisdom and the knowledge of God, which is more than any creature could possibly bear. Did not St. Paul, that outstanding teacher and the most sublime of all who contemplate the sublime, full of wonder and more than wonder at this, exclaim, *Oh, the depth of the riches of the wisdom and the knowledge of God!* You could not reach this— no human being, no angel, not all of creation could possibly sustain virtue of such weight or the weight of such virtue. Still, the thought of this—that is, of such littleness—considering the greatness of your own infirmity, considering the fluctuation of virtue in all people, considering that stability that is the whole—ought to bring about great virtue in you, so that, in this fullness, in this weakness, day by day, progressing and growing, you may make ever new progress and climb new heights, knowing that you yourself do not have the power to do this.[44]

18. Consider how little it is that human speech can really say, and how much it leaves to be understood. And if all the things God made were voice or speech, still what they said about God

would be little or nothing compared to what God is. So, make all things that exist be for you the mouth of God. And if one speaks, shall all the others be silent? No, when one speaks, all cry out and proclaim, ineffably, in one magnificent voice: *He made us and not we ourselves.* Ah, Lord, who has ears that can be opened to hear this inaudible voice! Ah, Lord, so intensely would such persons love you that they would be completely enraptured![45]

19. Consider how all things pass away and cease to be, how all things are changeable, and nothing is stable. But you, even if everything else changes and is in flux, do not harbor any change within yourself, for God resides in the things that are stable and that exist, and not in what is passing. But you, when you feel some change in yourself, acknowledge that you are participating in the things that pass and not in the stability that alone exists. Are you not sometimes eager, ardent, and full of fervor? And if sometimes you are not, whose failure is that? Is it not yours? Yours, to be sure, and then you are getting a taste of what it is to be a creature rather than the Creator. Ah, what misery is yours in tasting this. How miserable you would feel if you felt this in you![46]

20. Consider that the most important factor in attaining human perfection is understanding things not as they are spoken of, but as they lie beyond human understanding. If, however, it is according to the light of the intellect that one's affection is kindled, is it not sometimes the case that one and the same thing kindles the ardor of one person and leaves another like a stone wall? So it is that some people cannot stomach *that very light food*—it is called very light because, even though it pins down our human spirits with an enormous weight of virtue, it still ineffably lifts them above themselves into God. In this way our earthly habitation is made heavenly. See to it that you do not ever become remiss, negligent, or stinting in guarding your own heart. Take care that your spirit be not confined by any places or anything else that is too limited. Nothing should constrain the one for whom God alone sets bounds.[47]

21. Consider, since the destiny of humans and angels is the same: What is the most powerful act of the angels? Their life, their

supreme act, is it not the contemplation of God? Yes. The same, therefore, ought to be the goal and the life of humans, at least those for whom the Lord is like the foundation of the mountains on earth. And who is that lofty mountain, but you, Friar Minor? Look carefully, then, to see if this is your life. For otherwise you are dead, because nothing lives unless God gives it life. For whatever is not of God is only bread, and *on bread alone no one can live.*[48]

22. Consider and see that when you resist some temptation, particularly a suggestion from the spirit of fornication (which being so much more familiar and frequent, is just that much more difficult to conquer), no kind of resistance will suffice you but a perfect resistance, so that when God triumphs, you are stronger, having been tempted, than if you had not had this temptation.[49]

23. Consider that the same God of all, who created the angels, also made the tiny worm. But, among his great works, what is held to have greater dignity than the angel or to be more worthless than the worm? And yet he did not become an angel for you but became a small worm. Then that which made itself as if nothing in a worm, now made itself nothing at all when it brought that worm down into the dust. Therefore, let human pride be very afraid. In the end, will anyone find delights at the right hand of God in that blessed life, if in this miserable life they sought their pleasures in things other than him?[50]

24. Consider, and say, "Lord, Lord, I have not done all I should, and what I have done I have not done well; even what I have done, I have not done by myself but through you. And even if I had done all things well, I would still be but *an unprofitable servant.*" Is this not true, since your debt remains unpaid?[51]

25. Consider what is the surface level of your understanding of everything, and that as it is, you understand nothing. Why, therefore, do you spout nonsense before you even understand? Consider how, while we are celebrating our solemn feasts, the Lord celebrates for us. We celebrate the nativity, the resurrection, the sending of the Holy Spirit. But I ask you, on these feasts is the sun more luminous, the moon brighter, the stars more resplendent,

the heavens more serene? And more wonderful than these, is the earth with all its adornments more beautiful, the sea more fertile, the air purer, or the order in all these things more noble? The solemnities we celebrate before God are once-a-year affairs, but the one that God puts on for us is continual. Therefore let the solemn celebration that you direct to God be continual, as well. What did you say? If, here, where we are in *the shadow of death*, the Lord makes such celebration, how does he celebrate for them—and how do they celebrate for themselves—who are already in their heavenly home, or in that realm of the good spirits, where the true models of these things abide?[52]

26. Consider how Christ, by offering himself once and for all to God the Father, wrought salvation for the whole world, repaired the heavens, and brought all things to fulfillment. Therefore, my soul, think of how you would be blessed if you worthily offered to the same God so acceptable a sacrifice. How great is the salvation, do you think, that he can give to you, who wrought such salvation for the whole world? All these things are a great salvation, my soul. Consider how God is silent at the sufferings of the saints, how silent even at the death of his only begotten Son. But were any of these abandoned? Far from it! For Christ had handed over his soul before the sun hid the rays of its light, the earth quaked and delivered up its dead, and so on. And yet God did nothing at all, nor did any of his saints. For although they seemed abandoned at some point and in some way, in reality not one of them was abandoned; rather, God gathered them all in his many mercies.[53]

27. Consider that everything God has created has but one mouth that, though unschooled, is open, proclaiming magnificently his divine and multifaceted power. Watch therefore how you hear this voice and see if every creature is for you a mouth or a tongue, or if, rather, you have ears and hear not. Consider how, in everything, you should honor what is of God, such as in your living, your being, your capacity to reason, or in anything else. These things are marvelous, but more marvelous is the one who created them.[54]

28. Consider: If a prostitute, aflame with lust or with greed for filthy lucre (or both), loses all shame, then how much more, O my soul,

should you, enflamed with love beyond measure for your Jesus, lose all shame? In my opinion you do not love if you blush with shame or embarrassment. You miserable one, it is before the face of angels that you should blush, since you do not love Christ. What is a love that knows embarrassment? A paltry thing, I think. Blessed are those for whom all things taste of God. Blessed is the one who knows, indeed, that he or she is God. Blessed are those whose senses have become insensible and who are no longer endowed with sensation. Blessed are those who have so passed over into God that they no longer live in themselves but in the God who lives in them. These are truly great matters.[55]

29. Consider, O human, you who are lukewarm in your praise of God, how you take the very last place among all the creatures that the Most High made. Did not the Maker make things to praise him? Yes, this is what he made them for, and this is what they do. Does the shining sun hide the rays of its light? Or ever back off from its own proper splendor? Does not each star, and even the moon, variable as it is, keep to this same purpose? Does not the earth produce its fruit and do not plants do likewise? Do not the multiple powers of seeds observe their own proper limits? Does fire forget that its nature is to give heat? Test it for yourself, if you don't believe me. Or don't you believe your own self? So all these things, each content, as it were, with its own proper blessings, and grateful to God, obedient to their destiny wait patiently, as if saying by their very nature, that God is powerful and able to restore them according to their nature, and this is the way they follow him. For God has subjected them in hope. For he knows that they will be revealed, that when their servitude has been wiped away, he will reveal them in the glory of the children of God. In this hope, they observe the natural functions proper to each one, with which they were endowed. See, O wretch, how from the time they were set up, they have never even for one instant interrupted their praise of God.[56]

30. You miserable human being, you hold back, or you are lukewarm—you, I say, who are the image of God, on whom he freely bestowed his own likeness, for the praise of his unimaginable goodness; these [other creatures] magnificently praise God, and

never cease adding to their praise of him. Blush for shame, you wretch, and be confounded; and if you do not know how to praise him, ask them, for they are the ones who will teach you. O human, what do you think the angels or the good spirits did from the moment they were created by God, even while you find so much [pleasure] in these creatures that are far from him who is far from no one? And even if they are far off, they certainly seem to come much closer when they so magnificently praise the one who so much more magnificently created them. Blush with shame, you unfortunate human being whom all things accuse. Would that you could hear the outcry of your accuser! For they are united [in their accusation] who cannot be made one with him. You, who can be made one with him, cut yourself off from the one who is united to you. You spurn being united to Jesus who in order to unite you, you contemptible soul, to himself, willed to unite himself, great God, to you.[57]

31. See how miserable you are, for even now as you withdraw yourself from God, all other creatures approach him and draw near to him. Do they not condemn you? They do indeed; for they draw near in such a way as never to experience any movement in the other direction. Is it not unworthy of you to at once create distance from yourself and from God? Yes, unworthy and absurd. Weep, then, at this and say, O miserable me, because while I drift away, all other creatures are drawing closer to my God, although I have no doubt that it is said to me and not to them: *Draw near to him, that you might be made radiant, and your faces shall not blush for shame.* O my soul, by whatever least movement in which you do not tend toward God, do you not withdraw and fall away from your God? Therefore, since your digressions from the perfect are in fact not very small at all, they are doing you no good. The flesh says, How great is your hope, O my soul, when you suffer for the one who suffered for you! What am I saying? No, you have not hope, but a debt. And such a debt, I say, as can never be paid off.[58]

32. I acknowledge that the Spirit has spoken. Bring to completion, Spirit, what you have begun. I will speak, says the flesh, since I have begun. I say to you, therefore, that the more bitter these

things are, the sweeter to you is your Jesus. Do not therefore reject the bitterness because of how great it is; his consolations are greater by far. Do you not feel his sweetness even in the bitterness? Yes; I have told it like it is. The soul: O flesh, do not speak to me in this way, as if you think I am cold in my acknowledgment. For I have no bitterness, but even greater sweetness than you say. Keep your consolations to yourself, for I think they are deadly. Give them to whomever you wish, but not to me. I have the author of life, the consolation of spirits. I am more refreshed, even far more inundated with inestimable joy in these things you ignorantly call bitterness than you could be helped along by these contacts with him. Ah! How am I torn in two by the desire I have to suffer for him who suffered for me and the desire that I may long live for him who lives in me. I am in great agony, because I am afraid that if I suffer, his life in me will be ended. It is not the one who lives in me who harshly reproaches me, but rather I who reproach myself even more harshly on his behalf. But tell me, which of these is more agreeable to him, since I see that nothing is better than serving God and, in this way, it is good, even very good, to live a long time for him. Ah, what are you saying? Is it not better to break off life sooner, out of excessive love for him, and thus, as if breaking down the prison walls, fly to the kingdom of the one who knows how to love? Undoubtedly so. Remember especially, Father, these words from Scripture. *When one's heart is elevated, God is glorified.* What is meant by an elevated heart? Do you think that elevated things make the heart elevated? I don't think so. I say, that heart is elevated that makes each tiniest thing elevated. I say this because to me, even the tiniest things are extremely elevated, and if your heart is lifted up high by such little things, how high do you think it will be lifted by the most high great things of God! Note well what I have said, you who wish to be great. Ah! What power there is in these words. But it is hidden from the ignorant.[59]

33. Consider that the most excellent God made one most excellent harmony of all things, united in his praise. Isn't this what the word of God proclaims? *God*, it says, *saw all the things he had made, and they were* excellent, *very good.* And why very good,

excellent, if not because they put forth the very best, in the best possible manner? Ah, think how great God would be in you if from the furthest level of this harmony by which one ascends to God, you could attain the very summit. But what I have said is very little. You will have discerned a great deal if somehow you can understand anything at first. See to it that what you have received, that is, the things that are of God, all strike your heart magnificently. Bear with my ramblings, Father. For when I consider that I, who love my God, dwell in perishable flesh, I groan in all the depths of my being; all the more, however, I pray that I, who often lie prostrate in this dark prison, be led out from it to proclaim his holy name. For if I consider it unfitting for divine fire to burn in material so deformed, or for God's light to be sent into such darkness, I know, nonetheless, that the dignity of our God is great.[60]

34. Consider, also, lest in good fortune you lose the fear of God. For this is something that will last you forever. *All of us*, says that exalted soul [St. Paul], *gazing with unveiled face on the glory of the Lord, are being transformed into the same image from glory to glory, as through the Spirit of the Lord.* Look, what wonders! Don't those whose faces are thus unveiled, from whom the veil of human blindness is thus removed, appear to you as if God illumines their faces with himself? It is also said that transformation into the same image happens because one who enters into oneself draws very close to God. You have ascended very high indeed if you have entered into yourself, that is, become intimate to yourself. And what do you think it will be like if God is more intimate to you than your own inmost self? From what great darkness you will be led out by his spirit, and into what light! Ah! If you only knew those intimate states of contemplation that are to be found in those intimate or internal secrets! Would that you perfectly perceived those brilliant illuminations, those fiery splendors, those delicious—oh most delicious—sweetnesses, those peace-imparting savors, those things unknown and unnamable—but experienced nonetheless! What is it that thus elevates above themselves the minds of those who love? But it is too little to say *elevate*, rather one should say *deepenate*, or *otherate*; but indeed, not only whatever can be said is

46

too little, but also whatever can be conceived. Language does not come near these things, nor do the senses, or understanding, or knowledge. You cannot touch God, but he reveals himself most palpably, indeed more than any palpable touch, to the mind of the one who is totally turned toward him. But I do not think that anything that can be said about this is worth much. Ah, if you knew this from experience, I think that you, as well as I, could bear with dignity the dark moments of life! Ah, when—if ever—do you think, will I see? When, when, when? O the delay is too much, too much the heartrending postponement of these things! Ah, ah, ah, what am I to you, my God, or what are you to me? But what are you not to me?[61]

35. See, O human, that the words that you have heard are close to silence, so close that they cannot be heard outside of silence, because they cannot be heard except where they are, and they are within the silence. Therefore, enter into your inmost self, enter your own silence, so that you may go from your silence to God's, and his silence beyond thought may speak this to you. For the things you have heard are very great, although they came forth secretly out of silence. I speak not of human secrets, or angelic, but divine.[62]

36. Pay attention, O human, and if you wish to possess what you have heard, then do not seek these things where they are not. For they cannot be found where they are not. Outside of God or outside of silence, they are not. O how happy is the human being whose soul, in God, knows what it is to become God. Now, I would not have called you a human being, if the name of human were not one of great dignity. I must confess, nonetheless, that by this name you are also greatly humiliated, for it falls short of what you are, you who have been taken up to be on the same level, as it were, to such greatness, by his mercy. O Lord, what I have tasted of you has aroused in me fires of everlasting love— or shouldn't I rather call these things "not-tasted"? Yes, I think they are more like "not-tasted." Blessed are you who know what it is to be absorbed by them. Blessed are you, O soul, in whose desire burn the desires of everlasting love. Or tell me: What are you like without these desires? I know, very well, that you are

full of miseries, you are even misery itself. Why then, in such a state of confusion, why then, O my soul, how much do you think you can bear of the blessed contacts with God? Are there any eyes strong enough, powerful enough, sharp enough, or penetrating enough, to focus or hold a steady gaze in this blessed light? Is there anyone, no matter how strong and stable, who would not be destroyed by contact with him? Do you think there are any such? I for one do not think so, for no one's strength goes to such an extreme of stability. You have heard great things, yes, the greatest. Be awestruck, therefore, you who hear this, for I think it is great and awesome.[63]

37. You wish to grow, O human being? Then, follow John, Paul, David, Isaiah, Dionysius, Augustine, and the prophets, and keep in mind the chaste embrace by which, as in the Song of Songs, the bride is joined to her eternal bridegroom. Consider what it is, what it is like, however great it is, that thus takes place—yes, consider that, so that you may become like it. O God, guardian *of ancient mercies, God of all consolation*, who could keep silent and not praise you, except those who do not pay attention to your works? O Lord, you educate our souls in you while they are still like little children, so that growing gradually, little by little, through love of neighbor, they burn with ardor, and having grown by means of this ardor they are united in peace: united in you who are peace, I say—you who surpass all things, so that your peacemakers may also surpass all. Then when they have arrived at you, you do all things within the whole of yourself so as to bring all their imperfections to perfection. And so, from you, plenteous source of all good, from you yourself, therefore, may they drink most fully of the fullness of your bountiful light. Thus, when they are filled with you, with the zeal of your fullness may they make their neighbors after them full of your light along with themselves. And indeed, in these souls, O God our God, do you not crown your works? Are we filled with anything other than your fullness? Are we able to fill others from our own neediness or emptiness? And yet, Lord, you are so abundantly good, that once you have given something, you would not reckon it as yours, even though there is no other channel of

good. Let my soul love you, O God, not myself, but you. I have found the twofold way of charity.[64]

38. Oh, if you would come into my heart, O God, and set it on fire with your charity and make it flame with your love, so that it may burn with no other fire than you; oh, if you would make in it your abode and your house of delights, so that in it would be your bed of repose; then I would love you unceasingly and my heart would be ever fervent, going from itself, which is death, to you, who are life. Would, however, that you would come, not so as to permanently establish yourself in my soul, but rather to establish my soul in you: my soul, which is outside of itself for you, as if it could love you, its Lord, without you. If you wish to be loved by my soul, of which my soul is certain, do not go away, for as it follows from what is certain that without you, you cannot be loved, my soul loves you through you, O God.[65]

39. When you feel yourself falling away from God, always say to him, "Lord, if I could, I would will what you will, and I do not want to will anything except what you will," and this is very great: to leave yourself, enter him, be enraptured by him, pass over into him, apprehend him, be transformed by him, go deep within, to the cause of all, be moved in love into the silence, rest in blessed quiet, have a fleeting vision of God's infinity. Do not be horrified if I say fleeting, for he can, when he wants and as he wants, prolong this vision—he who has the power to extend the tiniest thing to infinity.[66]

40. These are, I think, Father, the ways in which the Lord manifests himself to whomever he wishes in this life of misery—although for the just, it is not miserable, but blessed. Be very careful, however, that no one among the uninstructed hears this. Hearing this spiritual talk could be a challenge for them, and, because they would not understand it, they would be quick to condemn it. Avoid their contempt, and do not give them an occasion for it, and because you have learned to know Christ in ways very different from them, hide this like a precious treasure in your inmost heart so that the beloved spouse himself, who has set up his tent in the splendors of the sun does not take flight from you. May your Jesus find his delight in your sun so that he may

feed there and lie down there as for a midday rest. Father, pay attention to doing these things. For if Jesus indeed takes delight in the splendors of the light of your sun as I have said, then it is impossible that you should be deprived of his delights, which are the greatest of all. But you, look at how the things are that you have seen; be attentive, look carefully. What you have heard is great, so great that hardly anyone has ever experienced anything greater. Do you want to experience these things? Then mark well: no one enters into God in this way who has not first gone out of oneself; no one is enraptured by him who has not first entered him; no one passes over into him who has not first been enraptured by him; no one apprehends him who has not first passed over into him; no one is transformed who has not first apprehended him; no one becomes intimate with him who has not first been transformed; no one is brought into that love unless one has first gone very deep into that intimacy; and no one is quieted at rest in the blessed silence unless one has first known that love. After this, God is seen. So even if there is some sort of vision in the preceding stages, the clear vision of God comes after all these. But as I have said: My God! What perception could ever be adequate for such a vision, when even the perceptions of the angels, who continually experience this vision, cannot experience it fully in this kind of love. Let those who seek it, Lord, rely not on their own strength, but rather give themselves totally over to you, so as to pass over totally into you. May they be helped by you, my God. Listen, my mind, to the Lord your God, and lift up the eyes of your mind to see his brightness. For he exhorts us to see him: *Be still*, he says, *and see that I am God. See,* he says, *that I alone am, and let there be no other God beside me.* And *who can make the unclean person clean? Is it not you, who are the only one? He, himself, is the one who made all things,* Scripture says, *and Israel is the scepter of his inheritance.* So, speaking most truthfully that which is most true about himself, God pours into the human mind the most perfect, the highest, light from light itself, and no other ray of light than one like this, God's very own, could more truly illumine the mind's darkness. *I Am Who Am*, he says, and *He Who Is has sent me to you.* With this ray, therefore, which has enlightened the eye of your mind, turn to him by whom you have been most graciously filled with light. *Let your face shine upon your servant,* and so on. And therefore, let all such light-filled faces—such as God, such as his creation, such as Christ, such as the Christian people, such as the good in this world—cry out to God, "O you who are! O you who are not! O you who are not! O you who are not, you are! O you who are not yet! O you who already are, that is to say blessed in the heavenly homeland. O you who are!" By that ray all things are made bright. For it is the light shining in the darkness even though the darkness does not comprehend it. By means of this you have, O soul, access into the sanctuary of God, thus you enter into the Holy of Holies; Jerusalem, this is your conversion to the Lord your God. Amen.[67]

III

JAMES OF MILAN

A Learned Friar's Impact on
Lay and Religious Piety

A Life Lost in Obscurity

James of Milan was a Friar Minor who came from northern Italy during the second half of the thirteenth century.[1] We know nothing about the precise date of his birth, his entry into the Order, or the major turning points of his life. Some identify him with the companion of the pontifical legate Gregory of Montelongo (1238–51), whom Salimbene mentions in his *Chronicle*, an early account of the history of the Franciscan order.[2] Depending on the accuracy of this hypothesis, one could situate the beginnings of his Franciscan life around 1250. We can deduce at the most that he had received a solid theological formation, because of his practice of the allegorical interpretation of the Bible, which was in vogue at the time. He was a fervent disciple of Bonaventure, which means that his formation could be placed before Bonaventure's generalate (1257–74). He borrows prayers and meditations from Bonaventure, which complicates the recognition of the paternity of his work. Although he is a very capable Latinist, James of Milan calls himself only *simple and poor of heart*.

According to Bartholomew of Pisa, another compiler of early Franciscan history, James was the guardian of the Franciscan friary in Milan around 1302.[3] This could be an indication of the date of composition of the *Stimulus Amoris*, his major contribution to the Franciscan legacy. Scholars do not agree on the place of his teaching as lector, since after his stint as guardian in Milan he is transferred to a friary in Domodossola, situated at the extreme edge of the Milanese

Franciscan province. It is possible that he could have taught theology there also. Being expedited to the confines of this province was not at all a promotion and could have been a result of his sympathy for the Franciscan Spirituals, the radical wing of the early Franciscan movement.[4]

After his period as lector, he disappeared from sight. His work supplanted his person. We know nothing about the end of his life or his death, which no doubt took place in the first quarter of the thirteenth century. Suffice it to say that his life straddles several pontificates and Franciscan generalates that were embroiled in the conflicts over the interpretation of the Rule and the growing tensions in and outside the Order. This time period saw the condemnation of the apocalyptic ideas of Joachim of Fiore and the persecution of the Spirituals by the papacy and the dominant wing of the Franciscans.[5] His work contains no direct reference to these conflicts.

A Work of Influence: The *Stimulus Amoris*

Authenticity and Dates

For a long time, the *Stimulus Amoris* was attributed to Bonaventure and other medieval authors such as Henry of Baume (spiritual director of the Poor Clare Colette of Corbie), and even Bernard of Clairvaux, either because of direct borrowings or because of a kinship of style and theology. The work was also associated with the Benedictine tradition and authors such as Saint Anselm and John of Fécamp, because certain fragments of their writings appear in versions of the *Stimulus*. It was common practice of medieval authors to copy others either totally or partially to enrich their works. The *Stimulus Amoris*, also known as *The Goad of Love*, experienced widespread diffusion in continental Europe as soon as it appeared in the thirteenth century, as well as in England in the fourteenth and fifteenth centuries. Several vernacular translations were made in Italian, Spanish, French, German, English, and even Gaelic. These underwent transformations and additions, which demonstrates the uncontested success of this type of writing. Walter Hilton, the Augustinian author of the *The Scale of Perfection*, provided a very free rendering in English late in the fourteenth century, titled *The Prickynge of Love*.[6]

Three ancient sources argue in favor of James of Milan as author of the *Stimulus Amoris*. First of all, in a manuscript written around 1300, one finds, "Here begins the prologue of the book composed by James lector of Milan of the Order of the Friars minor."[7] Later, a manuscript of the Library of Bergamo quotes the *Stimulus* as a work "edited" by James of Milan. Finally, Bartholomew of Pisa, who died in 1401, alludes to the work using *Transfige*, the first word of the opening prayer of the *Stimulus*. He presents the author as a "certain Milanese lector."[8]

The Franciscan editors of Quaracchi count 221 manuscripts containing the full Latin text and fourteen fragmentary manuscripts. Among these, eight are dated in the fourteenth century. Only one dates from the thirteenth century. The first critical edition was published in 1905 and reprinted in 1949. It is the original *forma brevis*, which is the shortest. It begins with the words "First of all, strive as far as possible." A longer version, the *forma longa*, which begins with "Come running, nations, from everywhere, and be amazed," was more popular. It is found complete in 221 manuscripts and partially in another 147. This uses the entire text of the short version, but it modifies the order of the chapters and adds considerable material drawn from Bonaventure (the *Soliloquium* and the *Triplici via*) and other authors, especially on devotion to the Passion. The *Stimulus* was one of the most successful devotional works of the later Middle Ages. Its popularity was only slightly less than the currently better-known *Meditationes vitae Christi*.[9] Our translation of the text will be based on the shorter and least-altered version.[10]

Destination

The prologue mentions a friend, "my brother John," as the one who asked insistently for a work of this sort.[11] He was, likely, a member of James's Franciscan community and his disciple. This enables us to suppose that the *Stimulus* was composed with a Franciscan audience in mind. Other indications, here and there throughout the work, confirm this hypothesis. For instance, chapter 12 addresses friars who have difficulty conforming their will to that of their superiors.[12] In chapter 16, James mentions the way in which very often one friar will have "to work very hard to acquire a devotion or some other inner attitude, while another will acquire the same attitude by the mere turning of his mind toward God."[13] But although the Franciscans are the primary target for this work, that did not preclude its success with a larger audience, laypeople as well as religious.

Literary Style

The *Stimulus Amoris* is a brief treatise of spirituality and Franciscan devotion. In spite of its rapid diffusion—and its great popularity in the Middle Ages—literary criticism has sometimes been harsh toward it. It has been criticized for its affective style and saccharine imagery, its longwinded passages and inelegances, its shocking graphic comparisons, and this in spite of the fact of its undeniable impact on Franciscan piety.[14] Although modern readers may also find it difficult, the spirituality of the book is sound and profound. The *Stimulus* makes available to the reader a sort of *vade mecum* to attain holiness in a brief space of time. For this, it asserts as a primary condition, "One does not need external work or health of body, but rather solitude, quiet of body, work of the heart, and quiet of the mind."[15]

The literary genre, then, is that of a treatise of asceticism filled with pious thoughts and mystical outpourings. James wants to offer "a method of how to live, pray, and meditate."[16] The book contains a variety of styles combining spiritual speculation, moral teachings, and affective meditations, most of which end with *Amen*. Throughout, the *Stimulus* maintains a didactic tone and an oral style appropriate for *lectio divina*. The "mixture of writing" expands the different levels of the literary genre.[17]

Structure and Content

The *Stimulus* anthology has no apparent order. It is composed of twenty-three chapters of various sorts, unequal in length.[18] The thematic texts of the prologue come from the psalms: *To You, O Lord, have I lifted up my soul* (Ps 24(25):1 [ESV]) and *To Thee have I lifted up my eyes* (Ps 122(123):1 [D–R]). This prologue discloses the intention of the author: "To show by a few meditations" how one must make an effort to seek God, come close to him, and "hold him tight in one's embrace." It concludes with a prayer to the Lord Jesus, related to the title of the entire work, as it pictures the core of the soul "pierced with the most gentle and healing wound" of Christ's love.[19]

The Passion of Christ takes up many of the chapters, a theme omnipresent in medieval piety and also among the Franciscans of the time.[20] This constant reference to suffering and reference to Christ's Passion is a clue to its affinities with the Franciscan Spirituals, who made it a leitmotif of their preaching and spirituality.[21] A passage in chapter 18 sums up James of Milan's version as follows:

> Tell me how can you claim to have compassion for Christ your leader, who died for you, if you do not suffer? And if you do not suffer, how can you be conformed to him? To be sure, if nothing else moves you, this alone should make you eager for suffering. What can be worse, or more deadly, than not to suffer together with the suffering of Christ, and to remain ungrateful for such benefits?[22]

The importance and efficacy of spiritual discipline is also a hallmark of the *Stimulus*. The last chapter of the work is titled "That One Can Become Perfect in a Short Time." In it, using the analogy of mountain climbing, James notes the distinction between the necessary physical and spiritual effort:

> Periods of rest are necessary when physically climbing a mountain because the flesh is weak. In spiritual climbing, because the spirit is eager, the contrary applies, namely, not to rest; when tired, one is to climb more quickly, run harder, and one will become refreshed and will be more anxious for greater things; so the climb will seem to be easier, more delightful, and pleasanter, the slope less steep, when one chooses to rest by not resting….Therefore, they are stupid and inexperienced in contemplation, who rest to regain their energies. They learn that in their resting they do not regain their strength, but rather lose it. If a

contemplative runs hard, it is pleasant; if one takes it easy, one begins to tire; if one rests, one loses strength.[23]

James of Milan concludes this chapter with the injunction to return to the Passion of Christ, whenever needed, as a sure source of healing: "If you are afraid of anything on the mountain, run to the cave in the side of Christ." If however, James continues, you find that, after all, you simply cannot forsake the valley of human misery at the foot of the mountain "because you were born and raised there," you can at least "go down there with humility on your part and compassion for your neighbors, grieving for your own sins and for the sins of others, begging God to forgive them."[24]

The *Stimulus Amoris* and the Motherhood of Christ

As noted, James's work was very popular in the Middle Ages; its influence is often neglected today. Aside from its contribution to the widespread meditations of Christ literature, in particular the Passion, it touches another important medieval theme enjoying a revival, thanks in great part to its contemporary feminist retrieval: the motherhood of Christ.[25] Chapter 14 of the *Stimulus* provides what is a very moving and daring innovation on this theme because of its graphic imagery.

An interesting allusion to this can be found in Jerome Poulenc's commentary on a stained-glass window that can be seen in the upper church of the Basilica of St. Francis in Assisi. This window played a key role in the conversion of Blessed Angela of Foligno, one of the most outstanding of the Franciscan medieval mystics. In the account of her spiritual journey, Angela tells Brother A., her scribe, that in the early years of her conversion, some five or six years after a vision of St. Francis had inspired her to turn her life around, she had undertaken a pilgrimage to Assisi, about six miles away from her home in Foligno, "in order to obtain from St. Francis the grace of feeling Christ's presence;…observing well the rule of blessed Francis, making her become, and remain to the end, truly poor."[26] After looking at this window, Angela fell into a trance and, once back home, she was unable to move for several days.

Poulenc describes this stained-glass window as follows:

Underneath the three angels of the bay on the left, the glorious Christ, sumptuously dressed, is represented standing on a pedestal. In front of him, St. Francis, about a third smaller than Christ, does not touch the ground and seems suspended in the air. The Lord holds him closely to himself by placing his left hand on his shoulder and sustaining him with the other hand at the level of his right elbow. The founder of the Friars Minor is dressed in the habit of his Order, and carries a book and a small cross. The stigmata on his hands and feet are echoes of the wounds of the Passion of the Lord and emphasize the theme of his union to the sufferings of Christ. The special vertical correspondence between the crossed nimbus of Christ and the cross of Francis further visually accentuates this participation.[27]

Poulenc finds the theological basis for this window in the *Stimulus Amoris*. As a result, he interprets it as depicting the spiritual motherhood of Christ. The reader must go back to chapter 14 of the *Stimulus Amoris* in order to understand what could have triggered both Angela's mystical experience in Assisi and the artistic vision of the pregnancy of Jesus with Francis, symbolizing his motherhood for all disciples.[28]

The *Stimulus Amoris*[29]

Prologue

...Prayer

"O sweet, sweet Lord Jesus Christ, pierce me to the core of my soul with your love's most gentle and healing wound. Wound my inmost soul with true, fraternal, apostolic charity, so that my soul may truly burn, grow weak, and melt always with only the love and desire for you. *May my soul yearn and faint in your courts*, may it yearn *to be dissolved and be with you*. Grant that my soul may always hunger only for you, the bread of heavenly life that came down from heaven; the bread of angels that is the refreshment of holy souls; our daily and supersubstantial bread, *having in itself every sweetness and every savor, every sweet delight.* May my heart ever hunger for you and feed upon you, whom the angels desire to gaze upon, and may the inmost being of my soul be filled with the sweet taste of you. May it always thirst for you, the font of life, the font of wisdom, the font of knowledge, the font of light eternal, the torrent of joy of the abundance of the house of God. May my heart ever court you, seek you, find its way to you," strive toward you, and arrive at you; may it meditate on you and speak of you, and do all for the praise and glory of your most sweet name, with humility and discretion, with love and delight, easily and effectively, with patience and peace and progress and perseverance all the way to the end; so that you alone may always be all in all for me, that you may always be all my hope, all my confidence, my riches, my pleasure, my delight, my joy, my gladness, my rest, my tranquility, my peace, my enjoyment, my fragrance, my sweetness, my food, my refreshment, my love, my meditation, my sustenance, my expectation, my refuge, my help, my patience, my wisdom; may you always be my wealth, my treasure, in which alone may my heart be fixed and firm and immovably rooted forever. Amen.[30]

Chapter 1. How a Person Can Make Further Progress in Good and Be More Pleasing to God

...Love poverty and all penury for the sake of Christ

Third point: concerning temporal goods, one should not seek or in any way strive after anything that is not absolutely necessary, but rather should work to conform to Christ our Head in poverty and in deprivation of all bodily comfort. And one should consider this the most important thing of all: that Christ, *the King of kings and Lord of lords,* deigned to put on the trappings of the lowliest servant and make himself be like the most stinking mud; and therefore the more anyone sees that they are rich, or have more abundance of bodily comforts, the more deeply and profoundly they ought to grieve, realizing they are that much further from the likeness of Christ....

Do not be indifferent to anyone who is suffering, but rather work hard to come to their aid

Fifth, one should not be indifferent toward anyone at all who is suffering, but rather be moved with a maternal affection for all people and thus feel deep compassion toward all, like that of a mother for her beloved only son. Treat all their troubles like your very own, and come to the aid of all, if possible, even as you would to yourself. And although in compassion and ministry you should consider yourself like a mother to one and all, on the other hand, you should revere them all as if they were your fathers and lords....

Prayer on the Passion of Christ

O Lord Jesus Christ, wound my heart with your wounds and make my mind drunk with your blood, so that wherever I turn I always see you, crucified; and anything I look at, I see red with your blood; may I be so totally oriented toward you that I am not able to encounter anything besides you; I cannot look upon anything but your wounds. May this be my comfort: to be wounded with you, my Lord; may this be my deep sorrow: to think about anything less than you. Do not let my heart rest, good Jesus, until it reaches you, its center; there let it lie down; there let its striving cease. Amen.[31]

Chapter 2. How Amazing It Is That Anyone Once Tasting God Could Desire Anything Else

We ought to be greatly astonished—indeed, we should be astonished that we are not astonished—how anyone, once tasting the sweetness of God, is ever able to be separated from it at all, how they are not so greatly intoxicated with it as to forget everything, even eating and sleeping. And if anything is put in front of him, how can they perceive anything there other than their most loving Lord, and, in him, enjoy the greatest sweetness, since they know him to be in all things and they can find him in all things, so as to find rest in all things. *Oh how good is the God of Israel toward those who are upright of heart! Oh how good and sweet is his spirit* in them! Oh, with what bitterness, what sadness, what anxiety, should the soul be filled that even for a moment is separated from such sweetness.[32]

Chapter 3. On Curbing Temptation Concerning Predestination and Foreknowledge [omitted][33]

Chapter 4. The Things That Lead a Person to the Quiet of Contemplation

...The second is to strive as hard as you can to suffer together with the Passion of Christ and in your heart to carry his Passion with you everywhere. Unless you know how to suffer with him by sharing his Passion, you will not be able to rejoice with him. But if you have pondered well his Passion, and entered deeply into his side, you will quickly come to his heart. Oh, happy the heart that is thus sweetly bound to the heart of Christ, *whose left hand is beneath her head and whose right hand embraces her*; then indeed the bride is properly joined with her spouse in their chamber. But, O blessed heart: tell me, I beg, the sweetness you feel; do not hide from me the delights with which you overflow.[34]

Chapter 5. Against Pride

...But, O marvelous, unspeakable, lovable mercy of the Savior, you who stoop with such extreme kindness to the level of our wretchedness! Who will ever be able to tell of it? O you human one, wrap yourself totally in his mercy, and marvel, and never stop giving thanks to such a sweet Lord. O my Lord, what have I done for you, that you should so sweetly touch and cherish me, me the proud and arrogant one. What is this grace that I have found that you sustain me in your presence to this moment? Certainly I have not deserved this; I deserve, rather, to live with the damned; more than that, good Lord, I do not even deserve to be called your creature. What could I do for you in return for all this, O immensity of goodness? What will I be able to present to you in return for such great favors? I cannot make satisfaction for my crimes, cannot work to earn your favors; I cannot even give you anything that is not already yours. I know what I'll do. I will present myself to you totally, throw my whole self upon your own self; always full of fear and reverence, as much as I am able, I will show you reverence; and if you see fit, I will faithfully and continually serve you. And if this is still not much, because I did what I could, you will approve it.[35]

Chapter 6. That Temptations Are Useful
for the Servants of God

O Most High, in your wonderful kindness you allow us to be tempted, not so that we might be captured but so that in fear we might flee to you, our most safe harbor. O Lord, you act like a good mother, who, longing to embrace her son who is at a distance, fills him with fear of something horrible, and opening her arms wide, receives her son fleeing to her, joyfully smiles at him, covers him with sweet kisses, and urges him never to leave her again, lest harm come to him. Drawing him close, she comforts him and finally gives him her breast. O happy temptation that compels us to flee to the embraces of the Son of God. O sweet Lord! You allow us to be pursued from all sides, and you always provide a safe refuge, so that with you we may be consoled at all times. Therefore, do not marvel, O human, that you have temptations; instead, flee in terror to God, and there, if you do not wish to be tempted, you will remain; otherwise, you can be captured and condemned. If, however, you have gone too far away from God and cannot get back to him, you will run to Christ, who is near to you, and in the cistern of his side you will hide, covered with a cloth. Do not be afraid that the enemy could find you there.

Always let this be your general rule: whenever you want your God to bend way down to you, carry the wounds of Christ in your heart, and, being thoroughly sprinkled in his blood, you will present yourself to the Father like his only begotten, and he, like a most sweet father, will fully provide for you. Go to Christ, therefore, and humbly implore him that inasmuch as it is not fitting that he be wounded anew, he might find it fitting to renew his wounds in your blood and make you totally red with his blood. Clothed thus in purple, you will be able to enter the palace of the King.

You who are tempted, meditate daily on these wounds; they will always be your refuge and your solace. Have no doubt that if you impress them firmly in your heart, there will be no way for temptation to enter in.[36]

Chapter 7. How One Should Set One's Thoughts in Order

...You should never harbor the idea that any sinners are so far estranged from God that they might not often, if not continually, turn to the Lord in their hearts, and that they might not then think upon their Lord more profoundly than you do and know him more clearly; that they might not attend to him with greater reverence than you, have greater shame for their sins, and bring themselves before him more humbly; and that they might not even be moved with more ardent affection in the presence of such great goodness.[37]

Chapter 8. How the Soul in Contemplation Is Inebriated with Love of the Creator

...O soul filled with love beyond measure, what will your beloved do? Will he be able to hide himself any more? Your most sweet spouse will come to you as quickly as possible. And you, seeing the one whom you have so very eagerly desired, will embrace him with love beyond measure, although always with reverence and awe. Then you would have every bit as much consolation as you could possibly experience, if you tasted it. But listen, most beloved of the Lord, once you feel safe again, he will again absent himself; and then he will be yours to seek with even greater ardor than before. What am I telling you? He will withdraw as many times [as necessary], until you are so worried about holding on to him that you never dare to feel safe, and everything now seems untrustworthy to you. But, O happy soul, listen to what your beloved will do for you! When you begin to be quieted with him, he will begin to give you the sweetest wine to drink. And, attracted by its sweetness, you will begin to be more moved, and he most generously will give you more; and you will ask for more, and he most kindly will serve you more. What am I telling you? You will not be able to be satisfied until you are inebriated and altogether flooded with wine. But would that after frequent inebriation beyond measure you may come next to sleep or rapture, if the Lord grants you to be able to experience it. For he is most generous and will bestow incomparably more than you could even believe.[38]

Chapter 9. How the Soul Is Inebriated in
Various Ways before Rapture

...Therefore you can understand that the contemplative person, however many other spiritual consolations one may have, still, before coming all the way to sleep and rapture (which few people achieve), is able to experience two sorts of inebriation. One is a kind of abundance of joy in one's heart and a fierce rejoicing (*jubilatio*) in one's mind, which comes after much weeping or much suffering with the Passion of Christ, or through great fervor in singular love of God from a new divine enlightenment of the mind. And this joyfulness so abounds in one's heart that it overflows into the members of one's body and makes them pleasing to the divine mercy. Then, from an excess of exultation, one goes about like a stumbling drunk unable to sustain the state of quiet, and one embraces the creatures one meets out of great love for their Creator. And you can well believe that then one's heart does not involve itself very much in earthly things; rather, encountering anything earthly, considers it all emptiness.

There is another inebriation that fills the heart with an excess of sweetness; this comes from divine companionship through the quiet of contemplation, and this sweetness abounds so greatly in one's heart as to overflow abundantly in all one's members to the point that one seems to oneself to be dripping with honey both inside and out. Just as the first kind of inebriation could not sustain the state of quiet because of joyful excitement, so this kind makes one quiet because of an excess of wetness. Unless this goes so far as to lead to sleep, it does not entirely take away the action of individual senses, but, as with a drunk, it does not permit them to be free. Then it is as if whatever you see, you consider to be full of a divine sweetness. And although the first inebriation is in an intensity of joyfulness and this in the intensity of sweetness, still there should be no doubt that the first also experiences sweetness and this one is not bereft of joyfulness.[39]

Chapter 10. That One Should Be Eager to
Do the Works of God [omitted][40]

Chapter 11. That a Contemplative Ought Not Judge Others Because of Apparent Defects

...If, therefore, you see yourself constantly intent upon spiritual things but others labor at other things, do not judge them, but acknowledge God's wisdom and benevolence. Reckon that you are weak and consider the others strong. For how can you reckon yourself strong, who, because of your very great weakness, cannot sustain the softness of a couch, that is, the sweetness of contemplation, but are moved by every wind, like a reed? What would you do, then, if you had *to build with one hand, and with the other* put the enemy to flight with a sword? Surely you would collapse from sheer terror.

Therefore praise the Lord your God, who places the strong in difficulties and adversities, makes the learned intent on their studies, sets up the compassionate as distributors of temporal goods. Lest you collapse, he willed you to rest in contemplation, so that you would not go astray; he did not wish for you to investigate subtle and complicated things, so that you would have simplicity; lest you be a bad dispenser, he willed you to deny all things at once so that you would be poor. Therefore, do not exalt yourself because of these things, but humble yourself; do not judge others, but exalt them. For these reasons do not exclude those who seem to you to be idle and unproductive; you should think how those who are wise and honest, when they acquire a fortune, hide it so it won't be stolen, working in secret and being quiet in public. In any case, know for sure that the One who *has weighed out the wind* permits them to fall short in those small and obvious matters lest they be lifted up in pride about those very great things God has granted them. And, although you should thus treat all those mentioned above, still, because you see they are in danger, you who live in quiet should pray for them, and if you are able, attract them to quiet....

When you see some people involved in temporal affairs, you will praise the divine prudence that provides by means of them for those who have attained quiet. If you see people involved in works of charity, in their case you will praise the divine goodness pouring itself out toward all things; if you see some people judging the rest, fear the divine judgment; if some incurring punishment, reflect on divine justice; if unyielding, fear greatly the divine rigor; if accusers and inquisitors, remember future judgment; if you see prelates who are remiss concerning punishments, in them you will commend the divine mercy. If you would have fervor, reflect on the extreme love for us of God the Father, who willed his own Son to become incarnate and be crucified for all of us; if you would be cooled, you will turn from all heat of misery and cling to that which cools and refreshes; and thus you will lead everything back to the praise and magnificence of the Creator. For there should not be any creature in which you do not pay honor to its Creator. In this is every creature worthy of all praise: that it is formed by God and by the same God is kept in being; and in this, that is called its being, may it marvelously praise its maker.[41]

Chapter 12. There Are Few Who Truly Obey [omitted][42]

Chapter 13. The Flesh's Dispute with God the Father Concerning Christ

...By means of all these things and others too (which I don't know and can't recount), Christ has much too greatly attracted to himself the soul that was assigned to me, and not just attracted it, but even entering deep within has pulled it away by his power to such a degree that he has already so joined it to himself with his coaxing that it does not take care of me, but instead it afflicts me, knocks me down, tramples on me, reduces me to nothing. And what seems even worse, it loves those who inflict these things on me, pours out special prayers for them, and if these things are not inflicted, it seeks to have them inflicted. So I am mortified, and it does not care; I lie in the mud, and it exults. But why does it add suffering to suffering and desire that I suffer intensely? It seems that it glories in being able to inflict upon me injury, contumely, and what it believes is most vile and burdensome. Thus it leaves me abandoned and afflicted, and it always wants to spend time with your Son, to be fed always with his flesh, to be inebriated with his blood. Wherever he might be, it wants to linger there likewise. Now it is found with him in the little manger, now it is embraced with him in the Virgin's arms, carried on the Virgin's shoulder, nourished with the Virgin's milk. Now it thirsts with him, now it is hungry with him, now spat upon with him, now wounded with him, now on the cross with him, and now in heaven with him it rejoices in your presence; now it grieves with him, now it is consoled with him; and wherever it goes, it goes with him; it does not want to be without him; it cannot turn to anything without him. What can I say to you, Father God, about your Son, because just as he has inebriated the soul given to me with love of him, so has he thus alienated it from me.[43]

Chapter 14. That One Should Gladly Meditate on the Passion of Christ and How Fruitful One's Meditation May Be

...O lovable Passion! It takes those who meditate on it away from themselves, and renders them not merely angelic, but divine! For if you spend time in meditation sharing the torments of Christ, you do not even see yourself, but God; you always behold the suffering Lord, you want to bear the cross with him; you carry in your heart heaven and earth in a handful, and for his sake bear every burden lightly. You want to be crowned with thorns together with Christ, and you're crowned with the hope of glory; you want to be cold with him on the cross without any clothes, and are made to burn with an excessive ardor of love; you want to taste the vinegar with him, and you drink wine of inexpressible sweetness; you want to be mocked with him on the cross, and are honored by the angels and adopted by the Blessed Virgin as her child. Wanting to be sad with Christ, you are made glad; wanting to be greatly afflicted along with Christ, you are consoled; you want to suffer with the one suffering, and are made exceedingly joyful; want to hang with Christ on the cross, and Christ embraces you most sweetly; want to bow your face suffused with the pallor of death, and Christ, lifting your head, very gently kisses you. O lovable death, O delightful death! Oh, why was I not in the place where that cross was that I might have been nailed together with Christ, hand and foot! I certainly would have said to Joseph of Arimathaea: Do not take him away from me, but bury me with him in the sepulchre; I do not want to be separated from him any more. But even if I cannot do it in this way physically, I want at least to do it in my heart. For, *it is good to be* with him, and in him I want *to make three tabernacles*: one in his hands, one in his feet, and yet another always in his side. There I wish to rest quietly and sleep, to eat and drink, to read and pray. There *I will speak to* his *heart*, and I will beg him for what I want. In so doing I will follow in the footsteps of my most sweet mother, *whose soul was pierced by the sword* of her son's Passion. Wounded, I will speak confidently to her about him, and I will incline her toward what I want. And I will not only be there crucified with her son, but going back even to the manger, I will lie there, a baby with him, so that in the same place with her son I will get to nurse at her breasts. And thus I will mix the milk of the mother with the blood of the son, and make for myself a drink most sweet.

O most loving wounds of my Lord Jesus Christ! For when I went to enter into them, as it were with my eyes open, my eyes became full of blood, and so, since I saw nothing else, I began to go in feeling with my hands until I finally came to the innermost viscera of his charity, and surrounded by this on every side I wanted never to come back. And therefore I dwell there, and what he eats I eat for my food, and there I am inebriated with his drink; there I abound in such great sweetness that I could never tell you. And he who first for sinners was in the womb of the Virgin now deigns to carry me, worthless me, in his viscera. But my great fear is that the time of his giving birth will come, and I will be cast forth from these delights that I enjoy. Surely, if he gives birth to me, he will have to nurse me like a mother at his breasts, wash me with his hands, carry me in his arms, comfort me with kisses, and fondle me in his lap. But surely, I know what I'll do: no matter how often he gives birth to me, I know that his wounds are always open, and through them I will enter into his womb again. I will repeat all this over and over until I am insep-arably merged with him. O the blindness of the sons of Adam, who do not know how to enter into Christ through these wounds! They labor beyond their strength in vain and the gates to repose stand open. Do you not know that Christ is the joy of the blessed? So why do you delay entering into that joy through the aperture of his body? What kind of insanity is this? The blessedness of angels is in sight, and the surrounding wall is broken down, and you don't bother to go in! Or perhaps you think that first your body should be got out of the way, because you believe that in its presence the soul could not man-age to attain quiet in Christ? But believe me, O human, if you strive to enter through this narrow opening, not only your soul, but your body as well, will find quiet and amazing sweetness there. What is carnal and attracted to the carnal will, by entering through the wounds, becomes so spiritual that it will regard as nothing any delights other than those it experiences there. What is more, the soul may even sometimes dictate that you ought to withdraw in order to be obedient or to be useful in some way, but the flesh, bound by that sweetness, will say you ought to stay. And if this sweetness is what happens to the body, how much sweetness do you think bathes the soul that is joined through that aperture to the heart of Christ? I certainly cannot express it to you, but experience it and know for yourself.[44]

Chapter 15. Good Friday Meditation

Standing by the cross of Jesus was his mother. O my Lady, where are you standing? Next to the cross? No, surely, you are rather on the cross with your Son, there you are crucified with him. The fact is that he is crucified in his body, but you in your heart; and also the wounds dispersed throughout his body are all united in your heart. There, Lady, is your heart pierced with a lance, there it is nailed, there crowned with thorns, there made fun of, filled with mockery and insults, and given vinegar and gall to drink. O Lady, why did you go to be immolated for us? Was your Son's Passion not enough without his mother also being crucified? O heart of love, why were you turned into a mass of sorrow? I gaze, Lady, at your heart, and I do not see a heart: I see myrrh, absinth, and gall. I look for the Mother of God and I find spittle, whipping, and wounds, because you have been completely transformed into these things. O Lady full of bitter sadness, what have you done? O vessel of sanctity, why have you been made a vessel of punishment? O Lady, why are you not by yourself in your chamber? Why did you go to the Place of the Skull? It is not your usual custom to go near such spectacles. Why didn't your virginal modesty keep you away? Why didn't your womanly fears keep you away? Why didn't your horror of criminal deeds keep you away? Why didn't the foulness of the place keep you away? Why didn't the crowd of rabble keep you away? Why didn't your hatred of evil keep you away? Why didn't the loud shouting keep you away? Why didn't the madness of fools keep you away? Why didn't the demoniacal mob keep you away? All these things you never even took into consideration, Lady, because your heart went out from you with grief: you were not in yourself, but in your Son's affliction, in the wounds of your only child, in the death of the one you loved. Your heart was aware not of a crowd, but a wound; not the press of the mob, but his being fixed to the cross; not noise, but bruising; not horror, but grief.[45] Go back, Lady, to where you were, lest when the shepherd is struck down we also lose you. Why in one hour should we be deprived of both guides? It is not customary, Lady, to condemn women to such a death and it was not on you, Lady, that sentence was pronounced.

But I don't think you can even hear this, because *you are filled with bitter sorrow*; your entire heart, Lady, was turned toward your son's Passion. What a marvel: you are totally in the wounds of Christ, the whole of Christ is crucified in the inmost viscera of your heart. How is this: That which contains is within that which is contained? O human, wound your heart, if you wish to understand this question. Open your heart to the nails and the lance and truth will enter in. The sun of justice does not enter into a closed heart. But, O Wounded Lady, wound our hearts and in our hearts renew the Passion of your Son. Join your wounded heart to ours, so that we may be wounded with your Son's wounds, the same as you. Why do I not at least have this heart of yours, Lady, so that wherever I go I always see you, joined to your Son? O Lady, if you are not willing to give me your crucified Son, or your wounded heart, then at least, I beg you, grant me your Son's wounds, insults, jeering, opprobrium, all that which you also feel within yourself. For what mother, if she could, would not gladly take suffering away from her son and herself, and lay them on her servant? Or, if you are so besotted with these things that you do not wish to remove them from your heart and from your Son and give them to anyone else, at least, Lady, join me to those insults and wounds, though I am no way worthy of them, so that you and your Son would have the consolation of company in your suffering. Oh how happy I would be, if I could only share those wounds with you and him! For what is greater today, my Lady, than to have a heart united to your opened heart and the pierced body of your Son? Is not your heart full of grace? And, if it is opened, how could that grace not flow into a heart united to it? And if your Son is the glory of the blessed ones, how, if he is pierced, could the sweetness of his glory not spread into the heart that is joined to him? I do not see how it could be otherwise, but I am afraid that sometimes we are far away when we believe ourselves to be close.

O my Lady, why do you not give me what I ask for? If I have offended you, wound my heart for the sake of justice; if I have been of service to you, now for my payment I ask wounds. And where, Lady, where is your loving kindness, where is your great clemency? Why have you become cruel to me, you who have always been kind? Why have you become stingy with me, you who have always been generous and liberal? I'm not asking you, Lady, for the sun or the stars, I'm asking for wounds. What is this that you are so stingy with those wounds? O Lady, either take my bodily life from me, or else wound my heart. It is shameful and disgraceful for me to see my Lord wounded and you, O my Lady, wounded with him, and me, most worthless slave, go on my way unharmed. But to be sure I know what I'll do: I will throw myself at your feet and beg you without ceasing, with tears and cries, and I will be a complete nuisance to you. You will either grant me what I ask for or maybe you will beat me to make me go away; but I will stand there and take your blows until I am completely wounded—and this is nothing other than the wounds I ask you for. But if you wish to soothe me without blows, I will persist stubbornly, and receive your sweet words, and your coaxing will wound my heart with love. Or, if you don't do anything or say anything, then my heart will be wounded with sadness and grief. And thus I will not go away without being wounded. Amen.

And all these things you ought to seek for anyone, and you ought to pray anxiously for them in relation to forgiveness from anyone. And when you see anything that is good in your neighbor you should be wonderfully glad, even if you see that you do not have the same good in you. Because if you don't do this, but feel sorry instead, you commit three very great evils by this sin. The first is that you appear to hate the honor of God, the cause of that person's good. Second, that you scorn the Passion of Christ, who suffered for this: that everyone might abound in virtues. Third, that you rend and tear the charity by which you should love you neighbor as yourself and strive for your neighbor's good as if for your own.

Therefore, may you greatly love your neighbor's good and look to both the greatest spiritual good, and also, when necessity requires, the material good, of your neighbor. And the Lord will always show you spiritual things and finally call you to the heavenly things to which may he himself lead us, who for us willed to undergo the shame of the cross. Amen.[46]

Chapter 16. A Contemplative Man Ought Not Think of Others as Being More Imperfect Than Himself [omitted][47]

Chapter 17. How One Should Incite Oneself to the Love of God, and How Greatly One Can Set One's Heart on Fire

...First, therefore, O human, understand that there is nothing that can set you so afire with love for him like the immense gift of his benefits. For insofar as you consider that he is so generous as to bestow upon you ineffable gifts you will reflect that he loves you beyond measure. And what excites one more to loving than to be loved and to be cherished?...

Therefore, approach him in this way. You should consider that you stand before God in a real, not a pretend, way; for where he is, he is, the same as he is in the highest fiery heaven; and recognize that you are his and not your own; and have no doubt that whatever you seek from him that is for your good you will receive, but God will not grant what you ask if it will harm you. All these things are certainly incentives for love. How could you not love him, whose own you are, and who is prepared to give you all things? Do you not greatly love the one who gives you something? And all the more him who gives you all things—nay, more, who even gives his own very self to you? If therefore you love yourself, in what way do you not love him who made you? You have ruined yourself and are still in the process of ruining yourself and yet you love yourself; and the one who made you and repaired you and preserves you, you do not love? Therefore say to the Lord: Lord, I am your creation, and you cannot deny me your very self....[48]

Chapter 18. To Love God Perfectly One Must Hate Oneself [omitted][49]

Chapter 19. How Glorious It Would Be and How It Would Be Possible for a Human Being to Be Transformed into God

O marvelous transformation by the right hand of the Most High. Think how marvelous it would be in the eyes of people who love temporal things if someone could transform one very filthy piece of excrement into all the delights and honors of this world. That is to say, you could have for one filthy turd total domination of the world, like the power of an emperor in temporal affairs, plus that of the pope in spiritual matters. No resistance would be possible, even evil spirits would obey you. And not only earth, but also the heavens and the stars would be ruled by your nod, and you could kill and raise the dead and cure the sick. You could even change the course of nature in all things and have all delights and riches that you could imagine (except for God), and, more than that, you would have anything whatever that God could possibly make (only not leading into God). Like that, only much more so is that admirable and praiseworthy and lovable transformation by which someone is changed into God. For the distance between a human being and God is incomparably greater than that between the lowliest creature whatsoever and all things that God could make outside himself. A person, however, is changed into God when one chooses to care nothing for oneself and to love only God, and when a person wills to be moved by nothing except that which concerns God. Such a one throws oneself only into that affection and is concerned about nothing except God himself, and totally thirsts for ways in which the Lord God can be honored by oneself and by others.[50]

Chapter 20. That One Should Willingly Give One's Heart to God [omitted][51]

Chapter 21. Attitude Toward One's Neighbor [omitted][52]

Chapter 22. That One Is Always to Be Well Ordered in Thought, Word, and Deed

...It is certainly amazing how such a little spark, like my heart, is not totally absorbed by the immense goodness of God, and how a servant of God does not always march along inebriated with the love of one's Lord. This, I think, would happen if one were determined to fasten one's heart to that immense goodness. It follows from this that no one should doubt that the more they would wish to fasten their heart to the immense goodness, the better and more perfect they would be. And those who are able to fasten their hearts on the highest good, so that utterly oblivious of anything else they strive toward that with a wholehearted effort, and there they rest not immediately pulling away from such goodness—then, I think they will be brought to the highest degree of perfection in an instant, absorbed in sweetness. Then they will walk oblivious among consolations and tribulations, vituperations and honors, flattery and insults, aware of nothing except God, striving only for God's honor. Then such a one can be called one who has arrived, rather than a pilgrim; blessed, not miserable; an angel, not a human; and not a sinner, but a saint.[53]

Chapter 23. That One Can Become Perfect in a Short Time

…When physically climbing a mountain, if people become tired halfway up and want to rest, they do not go back down to the valley to rest, because that way they would never be able to reach the peak and everyone would think they were very stupid.…

This is the reason, in my opinion, why so few of today's contemplatives reach the mountain peak. If people would climb today as far as they can, and rest there without going back at all, then tomorrow go up higher and there also get a foothold for their heart, and after that climb from there, and keep doing that, I tell you they will make more progress in a month than someone else in fifty years who goes back to rest and keeps returning to the same place. And I believe that these people in a short time would reach that state and be glorious in the presence of God and greatly beloved by the whole heavenly court.[54]

GENERAL CONCLUSION

At the end of these three major works of the thirteenth and fourteenth centuries, one can conclude that Giles of Assisi, Roger of Provence, and James of Milan are true disciples of Francis of Assisi and, at the same time, original interpreters of the Franciscan insights in matters of the *things of heaven*: "Blessed are the clean in heart, for they will see God. The truly clean of heart are those who look down upon earthly things, seek those of heaven, and, with a clean heart and spirit, never cease adoring and seeing the Lord God living and true."[1] They reveal their own understanding of the gospel experience while on the path to the God of Jesus Christ. The *Golden Sayings*, the *Meditations*, and the *Goad of Love* have marked their times. An attentive reader of these writings, whatever the literary genre may be, can both identify aspects of the Franciscan spirituality and unquestionable elements of the search for God. The works published here, completed with biographical narratives, are colored by a radical mysticism often expressed as a paradoxical experience of the divine.

Our general introduction addressed questions that remain unsolved in part because of the limited choice of authors: Who are these exceptional Friars Minor? What is their contribution to the Franciscan insights of the origins? What are the specific accents of their works? What elements have been forgotten? Why have they had more influence in the piety of the lay world than among the sons of Francis of Assisi? One can submit only a few answers, still open to interpretation and discussion.

Three Friars, Free and Marginal

Giles, Roger, and James appear to be free prophets on the horizon of the spiritual values of the growing Franciscan tradition; they reveal themselves as dissidents by their way of living and encountering Christ. It seems that the Franciscan movement quickly cast them aside once their work was published or their life testimony was used. Such is the case for Giles, forgotten by his peers after Saint Bonaventure interviewed him on the life of Francis. These authors are original in their teachings and manage to set their mark on a Brotherhood getting more and more institutionalized. They are authentic Friars Minor, bound together by a traditional questioning inherited by the Fathers and Mothers of the Desert: *How does one find God?* This monastic quest seemed to them more important than the new questioning brought out by the mendicant movement: *How does one bring God to the people?*

They still remain unclassifiable; the Spiritual tag often given to them because of their political stand is more than limited. They transmit a bold Franciscan legacy without referring to it explicitly, except for absolute silence on matters of God with Giles, the incapacity to name God with Roger, and the ability to give birth to the Lord with James.

The Primacy of God at the Core of Their Experience

One major feature of this anthology is the primacy of the experience of God's presence. It is a constant theme, not only in the authors' teachings but also in the description of their contemplative and mystical states. We have no other direct access to their experience than their teachings and their confidences. God's presence comes out as a vivid consciousness of his being. They experience this consciousness like a battling ground, and a constant need for vigilance and conversion. Feeling and knowing are also part of their apprenticeship of interior life. This is more obvious in Roger's *Meditations*. His vocabulary and imagery sustain a process of contemplation channeled through notions of *inhabitation* and *deification* of the soul. As Roger writes in his dialogue with the soul, "To leave yourself, enter him, be enraptured by him, pass over into him, apprehend him, be transformed by him, go deep within, to the cause of all, be moved in love into the silence, rest in blessed quiet, have a fleeting vision of God's infinity."[2]

The shared vision of God of these Franciscans is that of a path where one never attains the full knowledge of God, God being *ineffable, inscrutable, unimaginable, unchangeable,* and yet a path where one can enter into God's presence. For Giles the soul becomes a *dwelling* for God; for Roger and James, uniting with God eventually leads to being changed into God, *becoming God.* This evokes moments of *inebriation* and total *rapture* at times. We thus rely on Bernard McGinn's criteria for mysticism to better understand their mystical contribution to the Franciscan legacy: these writings reveal a deep *religious experience,* a *process,* and an *attempt to name the awareness of the divine presence*; we might also add, an eagerness to disclose to others the steps that lead to the divine presence.[3] Giles, Roger, and James also reflect Francis of Assisi's pessimism concerning human nature left on its own, a pessimism converted into a state of excellence once under God's gaze and love. As Giles puts it, all this fine talk about God remains *baby talk.*

The notion of God's presence, here and there, extends into another type of consciousness: the desire to follow Christ and to identify totally with his Passion: this is where their symbolism is at its best. The soul bears Christ's *stigmata,* and the self-offering of the heart requires us to settle lovingly into his wounds. Such a visual theme connects with the recurring theme of the Passion so dear to the Spirituals; it leads to the motherhood of Christ, as in the *Stimulus amoris*: "No matter how often he gives birth to me, I know that his wounds are always open, and through them I will enter into his womb again, and I will repeat all this over and over until I am inseparably merged with him."[4]

Forgotten Elements in the Legacy

Some themes dear to Saint Francis in his writings are omitted or seem forgotten by these writers. Giles, Roger, and James convey an acute sense of individualism in the spiritual quest of the soul; the Franciscan notion of fraternity in the *Rule* and the *Testament* is generally absent in their teachings. Their literary genres seldom refer to

Community life. The other, brother or neighbor, is called to mind mostly in the process of self-perfection. The notion of poverty, so close to life in fraternity in the Franciscan sources, is relegated to an ascetical combat and a private spiritual journey of self-denial. There are very few allusions to material poverty, to a life *sine proprio*, and the need to share with one another the bare necessities of life as expressed in the Rule. Strangely enough, there is no place whatsoever for the social poor. As mentioned earlier, such is the case for the lepers, so important for the beginnings of Francis and the Brotherhood. These omissions could be due to the fact that we are in front of a literature of individual perfection focused mainly on the soul's inner growth.

Father Paul Lachance advanced the hypothesis that for the three authors of our book, the question of material poverty had already been solved through a life of voluntary deprivation and penance, mostly in eremitical settings or in the wilderness and in secluded areas of the Community. It is as if the poverty theme, due to a chosen radical lifestyle, had become less relevant. It is a given fact that the poor material settings of most of the radical wing of the Order was a teaching in itself.[5] Therefore, the silence over the poor, the lepers, and the social outcasts in these writings is due to a privatized experience of spiritual life.

The Popular Success of Their Legacy

Giles of Assisi, Roger of Provence, and James of Milan contribute to the Franciscan movement in their own way. They convey values dear to Francis that became attractive to the laypeople of his time: the inexpressibility of God, how the power of sin is overcome by God's goodness, the need to tame the body and conquer oneself, the acceptance of vices and virtues as a constant battling ground, and so on. Each author enriches the foundational insights of the Franciscan beginnings. The gospel way of life is seen less as a path for the fraternal *sequela Christi* and more as a personal ascent to the peaks of the mountain of perfection. Very often, climbing new heights meant to practice spiritual caution and deal with inner paradoxes. Giles expresses it clearly:

If you want to see well, tear out your eyes and be blind. If you want to hear well, be deaf. If you want to walk well, cut off your feet. If you want to work well, cut off your hands. If you want to live well, hate yourself. If you want to live well, die to yourself....If you want to be rich, be poor....If you want to be exalted, humble yourself.[6]

The heritage given by these authors comes down to the bending low of the soul, through constant humility in order to journey into God and reside in God. Yet one cannot have access to God's presence without choosing the very same path Christ the crucified chose freely for himself. This is what this anthology hoped to reveal. *The Earliest Franciscans*, the book in its reduced final form, thus becomes more the spiritual legacy of Father Paul Lachance.

NOTES

General Introduction

1. *The Sacred Exchange between Saint Francis and Lady Poverty*, ch. 14, hereafter, ScEx.

2. ScEx in *Francis of Assisi: Early Documents* (New York: New York City Press, 1999), vol.1: *The Saint*, 529–54; hereafter, *The Saint*.

3. On the *Usus Pauper* debate, see David Burr, *Olivi and Franciscan Poverty: The Origins of the Usus Pauper Controversy* (Philadelphia: University of Pennsylvania Press, 1989), and *The Spiritual Franciscans: From Protest to Persecution in the Century after Saint Francis* (University Park: The Pennsylvania State University Press, 2001), 261–79; Malcolm D. Lambert, *The Doctrine of the Absolute Poverty of Christ and the Apostles in the Franciscan Order* (London: S.P.C.K., 1961); Andrea Tabarroni, *Paupertas Christi et Apostolorum. L'Ideale francescano in discussione (1322–1324)* (Rome: Istituto Storico Italiano per il Medio Evo—Nuovi Studi Storici 5, 1990). See also *La povertà del secolo XII e Francesco d'Assisi*, Atti del II Convegno Internazionale, October 1974 (Assisi: SISF, 1975).

4. The lay friars were outnumbered in time by clerics and priests.

5. This issue comes out very strongly in the *Testament* of 1226: "Let the brothers be careful not to receive in any way churches or poor dwellings or anything else built for them unless they are according to the holy poverty we have promised in the Rule. As pilgrims and strangers, let them always be guests there," Testament 24, in *The Saint*, 126; hereafter, Test. The warnings in the Rule did not seem strong enough: the *Earlier Rule* 7,13; 8,8; hereafter, ER, and the *Later Rule* 6,1; hereafter, LR. See *The Saint*, 69–70 and 103.

6. This meant providing food, turning to begging in times of need, receiving money for sick friars. One can observe an evolution in the care for the sick between the Rules of 1221 and 1223: ER 10 and LR 6. See *The Saint*, 71–72 and 103.

7. This meant clarifying the roles of *custos*, *guardians*, and *ministers*, creating gatherings such as local, provincial, and general Chapters, and forming new provincial entities.

8. Mendicant life, as opposed to traditional monastic life and its quest for God, was discovering its eagerness to bring God to the people, whatever the fraternal context.

9. Like preaching, administering the sacraments, keeping good relations with the church hierarchy, and missioning abroad.

10. On the question of the authority of Franciscan hagiography and the growing institutionalization of the Order, there is an abundant literature, out of which we retain the following: Felice Accrocca, *Francesco e le sue immagini. Momenti della evoluzione della coscienza storica dei frati Minori (secoli XIII–XVI)* (Padua: Centro Studi Antoniani, 1997); Stanislao da Campagnola, *Francesco d'Assisi nei suoi scritti e nelle sue biografie dei secoli XIII–XIV* (Assisi: Edizioni Porziuncola, 1981); Jacques Dalarun, *Vers une résolution de la question franciscaine. La Légende ombrienne de Thomas de Celano* (Paris: Fayard, 2007); Francesco d'Assisi, *Il potere in questione e la questione del potere* (Milan: Edizioni Biblioteca Francescana, 1999—Fonti e ricerche 13); Théophile Desbonnets, *De l'intuition à l'institution. Les Franciscains* (Paris: Éditions franciscaines, 1983); Edith Pasztor, *Francesco d'Assisi e la "questione francescana"* (Assisi: Edizioni Porziuncola, 2000—Saggi 5); Luigi Pellegrini, *Frate Francesco e i suoi agiografi* (Assisi: Edizioni Porziuncola, 2004—Saggi 8); Luciano Sangermano, *Francesco attraverso I suoi scritti* (Rome: Istituto Storico dei Cappuccini, 1995).

11. ScEx 15, in *The Saint*, 534.

12. ScEx 36, in *The Saint*, 541.

13. ScEx 6, in *The Saint*, 530.

14. True and Perfect Joy 11–13, in *The Saint*, 166–67; hereafter, TPJ. The Crosiers' place means "Go back to taking care of the lepers" or to the past, where it all began.

15. Father Paul Lachance was a Franciscan priest, member of the Saint Joseph Province of Eastern Canada. He was born in Lewiston, Maine, March 25, 1938. After joining the Order and being ordained to the priesthood, he pursued doctoral studies at the Pontifical University Antonianum in Rome. His doctoral studies established him as a renowned scholar on Angela of Foligno. He lived most of his Franciscan life in the United States, traveling between his Canadian Province and the Santa Barbara Province of California, while residing in Chicago, as a guest of the Sacred Heart Province. Paul was part of an ecumenical fraternity of Franciscans and friars of the Taizé Community of Chicago. He participated in the growing movement of small urban fraternities who wanted to get closer to the core of the Franciscan Rule, doing manual work, pastoral engagements, and living with the poor. After his doctoral studies, he joined a Franciscan retreat house in the suburbs of Chicago. From there, he lectured, preached,

accompanied spiritually, and participated at many international conventions on medieval studies. He then became a teacher at Chicago Theological Union (CTU) in courses of Franciscan spirituality, mystics, and prayer. Throughout his many engagements, he dreamed of offering an anthology of authors who continued the Franciscan legacy. The book was born in collaboration with a confrère and friend, Pierre Brunette, OFM, and with Kathryn Krug. Professor Bernard McGinn encouraged the project from its beginning. Paul requested a sabbatical from CTU in 2009–10 in order to bring closure to the book. He was then struggling with health issues. But his sickness and his premature death on July 31, 2011, slowed down the realization of the book.

16. It has been said, without nuance, that they are *a group of grumpy old men who did whatever they pleased*!

17. For Leo of Assisi, see *Scripta Leonis, Rufini et Angeli Sociorum S. Francisci: The Writings of Leo, Rufino and Angelo, Companions of St. Francis*, ed. and trans. Rosalind B. Brooke (Oxford: Clarendon Press, 1970). For Clare of Assisi, see *The Writings of Clare of Assisi: Letters, Form of Life, Testament and Blessing*, ed. Michael W. Blastic, OFM, Jay M. Hammond, J. A. Wayne Hellmann, OFM Conv., Studies in Early Franciscan Sources, vol. 3 (Saint Bonaventure, NY: Franciscan Institute Publications, 2011). For the *Privilege of poverty*, see *Claire d'Assise. Écrits*, ed. Marie-France Becker, Jean-François Godet, and Thaddée Matura, Sources chrétiennes 325 (Paris: Cerf, 1985), 196–201.

18. For David of Augsburg, see *De exterioris et interioris hominis* (Quaracchi: Collegium S. Bonaventurae, 1899); *Spiritual Life and Progress*, ed. Dominic Devas, OFM (London: Burns Oates & Washbourne Ltd., 1936), vol. 2. For Guibert of Tournai, see "Guibert of Tournai's Letter to Isabelle of France: An Edition of the Complete Letter," *Medieval Studies* 65 (2003): 57–97. For John Peckam, see *Canticum pauperis*, Bibliotheca Franciscana Ascetica Medii Aevi, vol. 4 (Quaracchi: Collegium S. Bonaventurae, 1949); and also in Saint Bonaventure, *Opera omnia*, vol. 8 (Quaracchi: Collegii S. Bonaventuriaie, 1898), 391. See also *Meditatio pauperis in solitudine*, ed. Ferdinand Delorme (Quaracchi: Bibliotheca Franciscana Ascetica Medii Aevi, Ad Claras Aquas, 1929).

Giles of Assisi

1. The initial draft of this presentation was given at the 34th International Congress of Medieval Studies, Western Michigan University,

THE EARLIEST FRANCISCANS

Kalamazoo, 1998 and published in expanded form in *Franciscan Studies* 64 (2006): 83–101.

2. *Scripta Leonis, Rufini et Angeli Sociorum S. Francisci: The Writings of Leo, Rufino and Angelo, Companions of St. Francis*, ed. and trans. Rosalind B. Brooke (Oxford: Clarendon Press, 1970); hereafter, *Scripta Leonis* for the whole book, and *Vita Egidii* for Leo's short life of Giles.

3. Arnold of Sarrant, "Chronica XXIV Generalium," in *Analecta Francescana sive Chronica Aliaque Varia Documenta ad Historiam Fratrum Minorum*, vol. 3 (Quaracchi: Collegium S. Bonaventurae, 1877), 74–115; hereafter, ChrXXIVG and AF.

4. "Historia Vitae B. Aegidii," in *Acta Sanctorum*, April, III, Venetis, 1738, 220–27. For a critical evaluation of the characteristics and respective merits of the three lives, see Stefano Brufani, "Egidio d'Assisi. Una santità feriale," in *I compagni di Francesco e la prima generazione minoritica*, Atti del XIX Convegno Internazionale, Assisi, October 17–19, 1991 (Spoleto: Centro Italiano di Studi sull'alto medioevo, 1992), 287–311; also, Stanislao Da Campagnola, "La 'Legenda' di frate Egidio d'Assisi nei secoli XIII–XV," in *Francescanesimo e società cittadina. L'esempio di Perugia (1276–1976)*, ed. Ugolino Nicolini (1979), 113–43. For a biography of Giles in English, see Raphael Brown, *Franciscan Mystic: The Life of Blessed Brother Giles of Assisi, Companion of St. Francis* (Garden City, NY: Hanover House, 1962). For a description of Giles, see Arnaldo Fortini, *Francis of Assisi*, a translation of the *Nova Vita di San Francesco* by Helen Moak (New York: Crossroad, 1981), 489–502.

5. Other minor sources for the life of Giles include Bartholomew of Pisa, *De conformitate vitae beati Francisci a vitam Domini Iesu*, in AF, 4:205–13 (the part relevant to Giles); Ubertino of Casale, *Arbor Vitae Crucifixae Jesu*, for which there is no modern edition, but the work is available in reprint of the 1485 incunable, with an introduction and bibliography by Charles T. Davis (Turin: Bottega d'Erasmo, 1971); hereafter, *Arbor Vitae*, 433–34; Giacomo Oddi (fifteenth century), *La Franceschina*, ed. N. Cavanna, vol. 1 (Florence: Olshki Editore, 1931), 259–73. Fragments about his life can also be found in Salimbene de Adam da Parma (thirteenth century), *Cronica*, ed. Scalia (Bari: Laterza, 1966), 810; Thomas of Eccleston, *Liber de Adventu Fratrum Minorum in Angliam*, in AF, 1:215–36; and in *Francis of Assisi: Early Documents*, vol. 3, *The Prophet*, ed. Regis J. Armstrong, OFM Cap., J. A. Wayne Hellmann, OFM Conv., and William J. Short, OFM (Hyde Park, NY: New City Press, 2000), 517–19. Unless otherwise indicated, all references to the early Franciscan documents will be to the three volumes of this edition: vol. 1, *The Saint*; vol. 2, *The Founder*; and

vol. 3, *The Prophet*, using these titles and the abbreviations adopted in each of these volumes.

6. See also Jacques Cambell, "Gilles d'Assise," in *Dictionnaire de Spiritualité*, vol. 6 (Paris: Beauchesne, 1967), 379–82; S. Vecchio, "Egidio di Assisi," in *Dizionario biografico degli Italiani* 42 (Enciclopedia Italiana Treccani, Rome, 1960), 313–16.

7. *Dicta Beati Aegidii Assisiensis* in Bibliotheca Franciscana Ascetica Medii Aevi, vol. 3, ed. Gisbert Menge, OFM (Quaracchi: Collegium S. Bonaventurae, 1905); hereafter, *Dicta*. A new and much needed critical edition is being prepared by Stefano Brufani, but its publication is not foreseen for the near future. For an English translation of the *Dicta* of Brother Giles, see Paschal Robinson, *The Golden Sayings of the Blessed Brother Giles of Assisi* (Philadelphia: The Dolphin Press, 1907); or *Golden Words: The Sayings of Brother Giles of Assisi*, with a biography by Nello Vian, translated from the Italian by Leo O'Sullivan, OFM (Chicago: Franciscan Press, 1966). For more current Italian introductions to and translations of the *Dicta*, see Eliodoro Mariani, *La Sapienza di frate Egidio compagno di San Francesco con I Detti* (Vicenza: LIEF, 1981); also, *Egidio di Assisi*, ed. Taddeo Bargiel, trans. Nello Vian, in *I Mistici: Scritti dei Mistici Francescani, secolo XIII*, vol. 1 (Bologna: Editrici Francescane, 1995), 79–169. We are indebted to Kathryn Krug for most of the English translation of the *Dicta* used here.

8. "Among the brothers assembled at chapter, not one of them dared to discuss worldly matters with anyone. Instead, they spoke about the lives of the holy fathers, or about the holiness of one of the brothers or how they could better attain the grace of our Lord." *The Anonymous of Perugia*; hereafter, AP, ch. 8, in *The Founder*, 53. For Chapter tradition, see also *The Legend of the Three Companions*; hereafter, L3C, ch. 14, in *The Founder*, 100–2.

9. For the existence of this oral tradition in the second half of the thirteenth century, see Ernesto Menestò, "I Dicta attribuiti a Jacopone da Todi," in *Le prose latine attribuite a Jacopone da Todi* (Bologna: Patron Editore, 1979), 90–93.

10. For the parallel between the desert in the early Church and the forest as wilderness for the early Franciscans, see Jacques Le Goff, "The Wilderness in the Medieval West," in *The Medieval Imagination*, trans. Arthur Godhammer (Chicago: University of Chicago Press, 1988), 47–50. For the infiltration of the lives of the Fathers into medieval religious literature, see Carlo Delcorno, "Le 'vitae Patrum' nella letteratura religiosa medievale (sec. XIII–XV)," *Lettere Italiane*, vol. 53 (1991): 187–207. For the hermitage and evangelization as "an inseparable pair" for Francis and the early Franciscans, see Martino Conti, OFM, "Hermitage and Evangelization in the Life of Francis," trans. Nancy Celaschi, OSF, in *Franciscan Solitude*, ed.

André Cirino, OFM, and Josef Raischl (St. Bonaventure, NY: Franciscan Institute Publications, 1995), 265–82; see also the two books by Luigi Pelegrini, *Insediamenti Francescani nell'Italia del Duecento* (Rome: Ed. Laurentianum, 1984) and *I luoghi di frate Francesco* (Milan: Edizioni Biblioteca Francescana, 2010). For the role of eremitism in medieval Franciscanism, see also Grado G. Merlo, *Tra eremo e città. Studi su Francesco d'Assisi e sul francescanesimo medievale* (Assisi: Edizioni Proziuncola, 2007); and Thomas Merton, "Franciscan Eremitism," in *Contemplation in a World of Action* (Garden City, NY: Doubleday & Company, 1971), 260–68.

11. ChrXXIVG, AF, 3:78.

12. *The Major Legend by Bonaventure*; hereafter, LMj, ch. 3, in *The Founder*, 544.

13. *The Life of Saint Francis by Thomas of Celano*, ch. 10; hereafter, 1C, in *The Saint*, 204.

14. In the Celano text, the following is added: "[Giles] lived a long time: he was holy, living justly and piously. He left us examples of perfect obedience, work, including work with hands, solitary life, and holy contemplation." The editors of the Celano translation note that this sentence is "an interpolation," since "Thomas could not have written in 1229 about Brother Giles' 'long life' at such an early date," that is, while Giles was still living; 1C, ch. 10, note b, in *The Saint*, 204.

15. LMj, ch. 3, in *The Founder*, 544. In his description of Giles in this passage, Bonaventure also adds that he was an eyewitness of his ecstasies: "He was so often rapt into God in ecstasy, as I myself have observed as an eyewitness, that he seemed to live among people more like an angel than a human being." And in another reference, "For thirty years he enjoyed the graces of mental prayer." *Sermo 1, De Sabbato Sancto*, in *Opera Omnia*, vol. 9 (Quaracchi: Collegium S. Bonaventurae, 1901), 261; hereafter, *Opera*.

16. *La Franceschina*, 1:260 and Bartholomew of Pisa, *De Conformitate*, AF, 4:212.

17. ChrXXIVG, AF, 4:205. See also, *Vita Egidii*, ch. 2, p. 323. It is also significant to note that this account provides major insights into the foundational experiences of the fledgling Franciscan fraternity at the Portiuncula; that the place where St. Francis lived "was near a leper hospital" (ibid., 321), and that, once he was accepted in the fraternity, "St. Francis took Brother Giles with him into Assisi to get a tunic for him," (the "tunic" reminiscent of the call to discipleship in Matt 10:19). In *Scripta Leonis*, however, the poor person in the above episode is a man, ch. 55, p. 185 (also, *The Founder*, AP, ch. 92, p. 195). For a close study of the divergent accounts in the hagiographical literature, see Luigi Pelegrini, *I luoghi di Frate Francesco*, 37–41.

18. *Dicta*, appendix 2, p. 112.

19. Giles was probably the first Friar Minor to make a pilgrimage to the Holy Land. See P. Golubovich, *Biblioteca bibliografica di Terra Santa*, vol. 1 (Quaracchi, 1906), 105.

20. See *De Conformitate*, AF, 4:205, 583. The same type of prophetic criticism against the Order is repeated by Francis to Giles in *De Conformitate*, AF, 5:160. Angelo Clareno will see in Giles the faithful witness of the primitive Franciscan ideal and prophet of the forthcoming tribulations of the Order. Although the source of his quotation is unknown, he writes, "Saint Giles, illumined by a certain and clear revelation, said, 'the attack is on, and there is neither the strength, time, nor wisdom to repulse it. Blessed is he who, giving ground before the enemy and hiding, can save his soul." See also Angelo Clareno, *A Chronicle or History of the Seven Tribulations of the Order of Brothers Minor*, trans. David Burr and E. Randolph Daniel (St. Bonaventure, NY: Franciscan Institute Publications, 2005), 115; hereafter, HTrb.

21. *Vita Egidii*, ch. 6, p. 327.

22. One of these first visions comes from the pen of Brother Leo in ibid.: "And, among the other gifts that God bestowed on him, one night when he was at prayer, he was filled with such divine grace and consolation that it seemed to him that the Lord wanted to lead his soul out of his body, so that his soul could see clearly with regard to its owns secrets, and could the better animate the body to work well and be strong in the service of God. And so he began to feel, from his feet up, how his body was dying, until his soul went out of it. His soul stood outside his body, and it was delighted; even as it was pleasing to God our Creator, who had put it into the body, because of the very great beauty with which the Holy Spirit had adorned it, his soul was delighted to gaze upon itself; for it was most exquisitely fine and brilliant beyond esteeming, as he himself related when he was near death."

23. On the initial assaults of the devil, the *Vita Egidii* reports that once in the church of St. Apollinaris in Spoleto, while Giles "was standing and bowed in prayer he sensed the devil come upon him, greatly oppressing and molesting him. Although he prayed vehemently he was unable to straighten himself but he shuffled along as best he could to the vessel of holy water and when he had devoutly sprinkled himself he was freed of the devil" (329). This scene is also reported in ChrXXIVG, AF, 3:95–96.

24. *Scripta Leonis*, ch. 71, p. 213.

25. On the early expansion of the friars minor in the thirteenth century, see, among others, Grado Giovanni Merlo, *In the Name of Saint Francis: History of the Friars Minor and Franciscanism until the Early*

Sixteenth Century, trans. Raphael Bonnano, OFM (St. Bonaventure, NY: Franciscan Institute Publications, 2009), 79–163; R. B. Brooke, "La prima espansione francescana in Europa," in *Espansione del francescanesimo tra Occidente e Oriente nel secolo XIII* (Assisi: SISF, 1979), 125–50.

26. *Vita Egidii*, ch. 18, p. 347; ChrXXIVG, AF, 3:78, and 4:207, 499; *La Franceschina*, AF, 1:263. The date of Giles's trip to Tunisia is contested. J. Cambell holds for the beginning of 1214, *Dictionnaire de Spiritualité*, 6:379, while S. Vecchio argues for 1219, *Dizionario biografico degli Italiani*, 42:312–16.

27. *Dicta*, ch. 25, p. 75.

28. The cardinal apparently offered Giles the option of eating at his own table, but Giles obstinately refused, preferring to eat separately and from what he had earned by the work of his own hands. ChrXXIVG, AF, 3:83–84.

29. "He stretched out his hand and laid it on the head of Brother Giles, the third brother, who at the moment was close to Brother Bernard," in *Saint Francis of Assisi: Writings and Early Biographies; English Omnibus of Sources for the Life of Saint Francis*, ed. Marion A. Habig (Chicago: Franciscan Herald Press, 1973), 109; also *Scripta Leonis*, ch. 107, p. 277.

30. *Vita Egidii*, ch. 8 and 9, pp. 331–33. See also ChrXXIVG, AF, 3:96–97, and 4:211.

31. ChrXXIVG, AF, 3:113.

32. *Vita Egidii*, ch. 8, p. 331.

33. Ibid.

34. Ibid., 331–33. The *Vita Egidii* often mentions Giles's reticence in describing his experiences of God. To the friar who asks him about a brilliant light that passed between Giles and himself, he replies, "Let it pass" (332); he also warns his brothers to "guard God's secrets and his treasure with great fear and caution" (337); in response to those who question him about his Cetona visions, he avoids any detailed description, concluding with, "It was not my fault that it happened" (341). In his insistence on keeping secret God's manifestations to himself, even though here as elsewhere Giles never explicitly quotes Francis, the affinity to Francis's *Admonition XXVIII* is striking: "Blessed is the servant who stores up in heaven the good things which the Lord shows to him and does not wish to reveal them to people under the guise of a reward because the Most High Himself will reveal his deeds to whomever he wishes. Blessed is the servant who safeguards the secrets of the Lord in his heart," *Admonition XXVIII*; hereafter, Adm, in *The Saint*, 137.

35. See *Vita Egidii*, ch. 8 and 9, pp. 330–33. Also, *Dicta*, ch. 12, p. 47: "If we were truly spiritual we would hardly ever want to see, or listen to, or

even pass any time with anyone, unless for a great necessity, but would always choose to remain alone."

36. *Dicta*, ch. 13, pp. 48–50.

37. Thomas Gallus is the first to quote Giles. On the influence of Giles upon Thomas Gallus, see Gabriel Théry, "Thomas Gallus et Egide d'Assise. Le 'De Septem Gradibus Contemplationis,'" in *Revue Néo-Scolastique de Philosophie* 36 (1934): 180–90. Théry suggests that Gallus was a friend not only of Anthony of Padua, but also of Giles. In his commentary of the *Song of Songs*, Gallus amplifies the seven stages of Giles, changing the fourth from *contemplatio* to *speculatio*; in *Thesaurus anecdotorum novissimus seu Veterum monumentorum*, vol. 2, ed. Bernhard Pez, 1721, 503–9. Gallus will have a considerable influence on Franciscan authors. See also Gabriel Théry, "Saint Antoine de Padoue et Thomas Gallus," in *La Vie Spirituelle*, Supplément 378 (1933): 94–115. On the influence of Gallus, see Bernard McGinn, "The Role of Thomas Gallus in the History of Dionysian Mysticism," *Studies in Spirituality* 8 (1998): 81–96; Jeanne Barbet, "Thomas Gallus" *Dictionnaire de Spiritualité* 15 (1991): 800–16; François Vandenbrouke, "La contemplation au 13e siècle," in *Dictionnaire de Spiritualité*, vol. 2 (1953): 1974–76.

38. The seven stages of contemplation are found twice in Bonaventure. First, in 1248, in his *Commentarium in Evangelicum Lucae* (*Opera*, 7:231), he refers to the six stages of Richard of St. Victor and St. Augustine, after which he recalls the seven stages of Giles. See also *Commentary on the Gospel of Luke*, Works of St. Bonaventure, vol. 7, part 2, ed. Robert J. Karris, OFM (St. Bonaventure, NY: Franciscan Institute Publications, 2003), 850–51. Then, in his *Sermo 1, In Sabbato Sancto*, preached in 1267 (*Opera*, 9:269), he expands the stages to eight by adding *amplexus* between *gustus* and *requies*. On Giles's influence upon Bonaventure, see also Jules d'Albi, *Saint Bonaventure et les luttes doctrinales de 1267-1277* (Tamines: Duculot, 1922), 186–87.

39. Giles addresses two cardinals who ask for his prayers, and admonishes them to overcome the pitfalls of wealth, honors, and power: "By these privileges you hope to be saved while I, wretched as I am, fear that with so many miseries and misfortunes I may be damned." He takes the opportunity to refer to the situation of "the bad friars in hell because they have not observed the Rule." Wadding, *Annales Minorum seu Trium Ordinum S. Francisco Institutorum*, vol. 2 (1221–37), 488; ChrXXIVG, AF, 3:87.

40. ChrXXIVG, AF, 3:89–90: "Brother Elias, immediately after the death of the blessed Francis, took the initiative to build a church of marvelous splendor near Assisi, on a slightly elevated site that was called the Hill of Hell (*Collis Infernus*). But after Pope Gregory IX, of happy memory, had

placed the first stone of the church of the blessed Francis, it was given the name the Hill of Paradise (*Collis Paradiso*). From this moment on, in order to finance this construction, Brother Elias began to impose levies of various kinds and had a special marble collection box set up in front of the basilica into which pilgrims could put money for this church. Faced with this spectacle, a certain number of brothers of admirable holiness and purity went to Perugia to ask Brother Giles, a holy and good man, what he thought of this fortress-like building and this manner of collecting money, as this seemed to be in total contradiction to the Rule. Brother Giles responded, 'Even if that house stretched all the way from here to Assisi, one little corner is all I need to live in!' As they insisted on the issue of the collection box, he turned to Brother Leo and told him, 'If you do not value your life, go and break that marble box; but if you want to live, don't do it, because it will be hard for you to endure the persecutions of Brother Elias.' At these words, Brother Leo with his companions returned to Assisi and smashed the box to pieces. When Brother Elias heard about it, he ordered his servants to give them a good beating and drove them out of Assisi in disgrace." On the role of Elias, see Giulia Barone, *Da Frate Elia agli Spirituali* (Milano: Ed. Biblioteca Francescana, 1999), and "Frate Elia," *Bulletino dell'Istituto Storico Italiano per il Medio Evo*, 85 (1974): 89–144; and Michael Cusato, "Elias and Clare: An Enigmatic Relationship," in *The Early Franciscan Movement (1205–1239): History, Sources, and Hermeneutics* (Spoleto: Fondazione Centro Italiano di Studi sull'Alto Medioevo), 407–20.

41. Angelo Clareno reports the complaint, unfounded in his opinion, that Elias had presented evidence before Pope Gregory concerning the evil ways of some friars who, "ruling themselves according to their own sense, have spurned the rein of holy obedience and have run about hither and yon as if they were headless" (HTrb, 74).

42. Reported in *De Conformitate*, AF, 4:208.

43. *Dicta*, ch. 16, p. 55. The Poor Clares were witnesses to a sermon addressed to them by the theologian Alexander of Hales that was interrupted by Giles. He insisted on preaching, and did so with an overflow of the Spirit, before allowing the guest preacher to resume his sermon. Clare apparently was very edified by Giles's conduct: "I tell you, Brothers, that this master has edified me more than if I had seen him bringing the dead back to life" (*De Conformitate*, AF, 4:208). On the dangers of knowledge, see *La Franceschina*, AF, 1:268).

44. *Dicta*, appendix 1, p. 91; taken up in AF, 2:86, and in *La Franceschina*, AF, 1:268.

45. *Dicta*, appendix 1, p. 91. Echoes of this salvo reached the Provincial Chapter in England in 1238: "Brother Richard of Cornwall gave a course of

lectures on the *'Sentences,'* in Paris, where he was acclaimed a great and admirable philosopher. When this Richard came to England he told in the chapter at Oxford how, when a brother at Paris was caught up in ecstasy, it seemed to him that Brother Giles, a lay brother but a contemplative, sat and lectured on the seven authentic petitions of the Lord's prayer, all his hearers being brothers who were lectors in the Order. But St. Francis, entering, first stood silent, then exclaimed in these words: 'Oh how shameful it is for you that such a lay brother should exceed your merits in heaven above. And because,' he went on, 'knowledge puffs up, but charity edifies, many brother clerics are counted as nothing in the eternal kingdom of God.'" "The Chronicle of Brother Thomas of Eccleston: The Coming of the Friars Minor to England," in *XIIIth Century Chronicles*, trans. Placid Herman, OFM (Chicago: Franciscan Herald Press, 1961), 144–45. See also, Jacopone da Todi: "That's the way it is—not a shred left of the spirit of the Rule! In sorrow and grief I see Paris demolish Assisi, stone by stone. With all their theology they've led the Order down a crooked path." *Jacopone da Todi: The Lauds,* trans. Serge and Elizabeth Hughes (New York: Paulist Press, 1982), 123. Critics disagree on whether it was Giles or Jacopone who was the first to fire this salvo. See Antonio Montefusco, "Jacopone Spirituale," in *Iacopone nell'Umbria del due-trecento, un'alternativa francescana* (Rome: Istituto storico dei Cappucini, 2006), 87n66. For Giles's position against studies, see *Dicta*, ch. 16, pp. 55–57. *The Chronicle of the XXIV Generals* also relates the confrontation between Giles and Bonaventure on the relationship between science and the love of God (ChrXXIVG, AF, 3:101).

46. ChrXXIVG, AF, 3:86. Clareno reports an even more stringent protest: "Saint Giles, the third brother to enter the Order, illumined by certain clear revelations, said, 'The attack is on, and there is neither the strength, time nor wisdom to repulse it. Blessed is he who, giving ground before the enemy and hiding, can save his soul'" (HTrb, 115).

47. *Arbor Vitae*, vol. 3, p. 433. In ChrXXIVG, AF, 3: 87, "Giles tells a brother who is astonished that he has not seen more Friars Minor in his vision of hell, that it is because he had not gone low enough, to where the brothers who did not observe or practice the Rule were to be found."

48. *Dicta*, ch. 19, p. 63.

49. ChrXXIVG, AF, 4:59. *Dicta*, appendix 1, p. 108.

50. *Vita Egidii*, ch. 8, p. 331.

51. Ibid., ch. 12, p. 337.

52. Ibid., ch. 13, p. 338.

53. Ibid., ch. 14, p. 341.

54. Giles was often seen in a state of ecstasy. One report has it that

"often he was seen lifted entirely up, a cubit and a half off the ground." ChrXXIVG, AF, 3:98.

55. Accused of being a follower of the apocalyptic ideas of Joachim of Fiore, John of Parma was deposed from his generalate in 1257. See *Giovanni da Parma e la grande speranza*, ed. Alvaro Caciotti and Maria Melli (Milano: Edizioni Biblioteca Francescana, 2008). Clareno also makes reference to Giles rejoicing over the election of John of Parma as minister general and as the man who would attempt but find "impossible the restoration of the 'holy way of life begun by Saint Francis': Brother Giles, inspired by the Spirit like a seer of future things, said: 'It is good and fitting that you have come, but you have come too late.'" This statement, quoted by Clareno, appears in none of the basic *Lives*. See ChrXXIVG, 3:95 and 83.

56. He had been visited by Pope Gregory IX (1234), in whose presence Giles "immediately fell into a trance" (ChrXXIVG, AF, 3:104–5). From 1240 on, he was visited by the provincial and minister generals, including Bonaventure (ibid., 101); by Lady Jacoba of Settesoli (ibid., 102); by other friars, in particular, a certain Gerardino (ibid., 102–3, and 4:210–); and by various preachers (ibid., vol. 3, p. 109). He also meets Leo, Bernard, and James of Massa, and visits Clare (ibid., vol. 3, p. 110).

57. *Arbor Vitae*, vol. 5, p. 433.

58. For a current review of this literature, see, among others, Jacques Dalarun, *The Misadventure of Francis of Assisi: Toward a Historical Use of the Franciscan Legends*, trans. Edward Hagman, OFM Cap. (St. Bonaventure, NY: Franciscan Institute Publications, 2002), esp. 175–204.

59. Bonaventure only speaks about Giles's contemplative dimension. He says nothing about his experience of manual labor or his itinerancy, and least of all, his role in the dispute between the Spirituals and the Community. See LMj, ch. 3, in *The Founder*, 544. Bonaventure will influence his secretary Bernard of Besse's vision of Giles in his "A Book of the Praises of Saint Francis," in *The Prophet*, 33.

60. LMj, ch. 3, in *The Founder*, 544.

61. ChrXXIVG, AF, 3:101; *La Franceschina*, 1:282.

62. ChrXXIVG, AF, 3:98.

63. *Vita Egidii*, ch. 15, p. 343.

64. Ibid., ch. 16, p. 345.

65. Ibid., ch. 17, pp. 345–47.

66. Ibid., ch. 18, p. 347.

67. On this sarcophagus, see ChrXXIVG, AF, 3:114–15.

68. When the dying Giles heard that the citizens of Perugia wanted to retain him by force so that his relics would remain in their city, he is reported to have said, "Tell the Perugians that the bells shall never ring for

my canonization, or because of any great miracle of mine; no sign will be given them except that of Jonas." ChrXXIV, AF, 3:114–15.

69. *De Conformitate*, AF, 4:212–13.

70. The *Vita Egidii* concludes with a summary of his qualities: "Seven highly praiseworthy and salutary qualities were manifest in blessed Giles. From the beginning of his conversion right until the day of his death he grew more and more perfect, for which reason we believe God multiplied the favor of his grace with a bountiful hand and gave him gifts with power fully and abundantly. First, he was sincere, a man of the greatest faith and catholic; second he was reverent; third, devout; fourth, dutiful and compassionate; fifth, careful; sixth, obedient; seventh, most pleasing to God and to men for the gifts that were granted to him" (ch. 20, p. 349).

71. Concerning Giles's importance, Giovanni Miccoli, in his acclaimed history of the Franciscan Order, affirms the following: "Bernard of Quintavalle, Angelo, Rufino, Giles, Leo, and others were the first protagonists of a resistance that the official historiography of the Order had, to all extent and purposes, cancelled out or dispersed," further emphasizing, "Given such a prospective, the refusal of gospel simplicity and mobility, manual labor and itinerant mendicancy, prayer and contemplation, by the dominant culture. The *Vita Beati fratris Aegidii*, provides a classic example." In "La storia religiosa," in *Storia d'Italia* (Torino: Einaudi, 1974), 779. Strangely enough, nonetheless, Giles hardly mentions the poor of his time, and while the sayings in *Dicta*, chapters 9 and 20, elaborate on the virtues of chastity and obedience, there are no chapters dedicated specifically to poverty.

72. The picture of Giles as mystic comes out more clearly in the eyewitness accounts mentioned in the *Vitae* and the various chronicles than in his own personal revelations on the subject. He is more concerned with praxis than with theory. His teachings on prayer and the path to attain the experience of God have priority in his *Dicta* (e.g., chs. 2, 4, 5, 7, 12, 13, 15, 23, 24, and 26). The four chapters that treat, explicitly, prayer and contemplation (12, 13, 23, 24) assemble, by themselves alone, twenty-seven *Dicta*, including the longest ones of the entire collection in the critical edition; they also have a clearly apophatic bent (e.g., *Dicta*, ch. 15, p. 54). Giles knew Francis's Paraphrase of the Our Father by heart and chanted it so often that one might sometimes think he had composed it himself. Cf. Kajetan Esser, "Die dem Hl. Franziskus von Assisi zugeschriebene Expositio in Pater Noster," in *Studien zu den Opuscula des hl. Franziskus von Assisi*, ed. E. Kurten and Isidoro de Villapadierna, Subsidia Scientifica Franciscalia 4 (Rome: Istituto Storico dei Frati Cappucini, 1973), esp. 227n11. Damien Vorreux thinks that Francis very early adapted the paraphrase of the Pater

to help the first brothers, nearly all lay brothers, to pray. See *Saint François d'Assise, Documents* (Paris: Éditions Franciscaines, 1968), 131.

73. *Vita Egidii*, ch. 18, p. 347; ChrXXIVG, AF, 3:113.

74. ChrXXIVG, AF, 3:86.

75. *Prologus* in *Dicta*, 1–2.

76. *Dicta*, 4–5.

77. Ibid., 6–8.

78. Ibid., 10–11.

79. Ibid., 12–13, 14.

80. Ibid., 15–17.

81. Giles calls to mind a mystical paradox: Mary is deprived of her bodily senses while becoming totally present to the Lord. The more she loses touch with her sister's complaint and her capacity to react or feel anything, the more she hears and tastes his word. The more she loses sight of herself, and the more she becomes aware of the Lord's presence. Idle at his feet, she becomes united with him. Giles considers Mary's attitude as the only work and true self-conquest that counts in comparison with the tribulations of life.

82. *Dicta*, 18, 19, 20, 21, 22–23.

83. Ibid., 24, 25, 26, 27, 28.

84. Ibid., 29, 30.

85. Ibid., 31, 32, 34.

86. Ibid., 36–37, 38–39; ChrXXIVG, AF, 3:93–94.

87. Ibid., 40.

88. Ibid., 41, 42–43, 44–45, 47; references to Isa 58:7; Matt 25:35ff; John 4:23; ChrXXIVG, AF, 3:87, 78.

89. *Dicta*, 48–50; references to ChrXXIVG, AF, 3:107; Song 1:3; Pss 33:9; 16:15; Luke 1:39ff.

90. *Dicta*, 51–52; references to Luke 10:41ff; Exod 25:4; and 1 Sam 16:7.

91. *Dicta*, 53, 54; references to Mal 3:6 and Heb 1:12.

92. *Dicta*, 55–57.

93. Ibid., 58–59.

94. Ibid., 60–61.

95. Ibid., 62, 64.

96. Ibid., 65–67.

97. Ibid., 68.

98. Ibid., 69.

99. Ibid., 70–71.

100. Ibid., 72–74; references to John 4:24 and Gregory the Great, *Homilies on the Gospels*, 37.1, PL 76:1626.

101. *Dicta*, 75.

102. Ibid., 76–77. There follow, 79–120, two appendixes not translated here: appendix I—(1) *Ex codicibus classis A*: *De timore Dei*; (2) *Ex codicibus classis B*; (3) and (4) *Ex codicibus 1/73* and *1/63* from Saint Isidore; (5) *Ex codice 590* from Assisi; (6) from *De Conformitate* by Bartholomew of Pisa; and appendix II (no subtitles).

Roger of Provence

1. The account of Roger's ecstatic preaching comes from the main source for his biography by Brother Raymond Petri: "De venerabili frater Rogerio, O.S.Fr.," in *Codicum Hagiographicorum Bibliothecae Regiae Bruxellensis*, Pars I. Codices Latini Membranei, vol. 1, Ediderunt Hagiographi Bollandiani (Brussels: Analect. Boll., 1886), ch. 16, p. 358; hereafter, *Vita*.

2. The Bollandists, in their 1886 edition of the *Vita*, refer to a fifteenth-century manuscript (Codex 2864-71) when introducing the lives of the Blessed Angela of Foligno and Brother Roger. See *Vita*, 346–47. The English translation of the *Vita* is from Paul Lachance and Pierre Brunette. For Brother Raymond, as *custos* and *pater*, see *Vita*, ch. 10, p. 354. See also Claude Carozzi, "Extases et visions chez Roger de Provence," in *Cahiers de Fanjeaux* 27 (Fanjeaux: Privat, 1992), 82. The second source for Roger's life is Arnold of Sarrant, "Chronica XXIV Generalium," in *Analecta Francescana sive Chronica Aliaque Varia Documenta ad Historiam Fratrum Minorum*, vol. 3 (Quaracchi: Collegium S. Bonaventurae, 1877), 383–92; hereafter, ChrXXIVG and AF. See also F. Vernet, "Biographies spirituelles: XIIIe siècle," in *Dictionnaire de Spiritualité*, vol. 1 (Paris: Beauchesne, 1937), 1666–67. His ecstatic preaching mentioned previously can also be found in ChrXXIVG, AF, 3:386. Both sources give an interesting example of "collusion" between the hagiographer and the saint, or the confessor and his confidant. Raymond not only collected Roger's confessions, he was also a direct witness to his many ecstatic episodes.

3. ChrXXIVG, AF, 3:382.

4. For his sojourns in Avignon, Tarascon, and Narbonne, see *Vita*, ch. 13, p. 356; ch. 14, p. 356; and ch. 19, p. 360.

5. *Vita*, ch. 15, p. 358: he studied the *De Trinitate* and the *Confessions* of Saint Augustine, and Hugh of Saint Victor's commentaries of the *Celestial Hierarchy* of Pseudo-Dionysius.

6. His radical change, the temptation that followed, and his experience of total mercy are in *Vita*, ch. 2, pp. 348–49.

7. *Vita*, ch. 3, p. 349. See also *Cahiers de Fanjeaux*, 27, p. 86.

8. Modern psychology would classify him as compulsive with histrionic (or hysterical) personality disorders. He would express exaggerated emotions, with loud and inappropriate behavior, torn between his visions and his states of depression. It is as if the highest peaks of ecstasy balanced his bouts of scrupulosity and his pathological sense of guilt.

9. His favorite mantras are, "My strength is enflamed in poverty," "Lord, my total will and salvation, out of which everything grows," and "Go back to your rest, my soul, for the Lord has done you good!" See *Vita*, ch. 10, p. 355.

10. On his practice of sense control and his elevation of the mind to God, see *Vita*, ch. 4, pp. 350–51. There is a link between the elevation of his mind, his physical *fervor*, and his experience of illumination. See *Cahiers de Fanjeaux*, 27, p. 90.

11. "Et propterea, inquit, mens quae Deum diligit ita tarde declinaret scienter ad venialissimum peccatum de mundo sicut ad mortalissimum," *Vita*, ch. 4, p. 351.

12. *Vita*, ch. 11, p. 355.

13. *Cahiers de Fanjeaux*, 27, p. 93.

14. The Holy Week ecstasy is reported in *Vita*, ch. 8, p. 353, and ch. 10, pp. 354–55.

15. *Vita*, ch. 7, p. 352.

16. Here is an example of a vision adorned with images, symbols, saintly figures, and dialogue, reported by Raymond: "Once, during prayer, he was raptured in this manner. He found himself in a temple of great beauty, the temple of the Trinity. There he saw an angel coming down from heaven. Getting closer to the ground, the angel flew softly around Brother Roger. After having circled him, the angel emitted enough smoke to cover both the ground and the temple; it became impossible to see the other beautiful angels present or even notice the tip of their wings. Still moving in a circle, the angel flew back to heaven. Brother Roger was then raptured into heaven, remaining still not inside but on the outside. And he wondered how such a heavy body could stay suspended weightless. And while he was in this position, a great opening in heaven occurred near him. He said his soul felt so much joy at the sight that he was not able to talk or express himself. And whenever something of the sort happened, he felt the same. The outcome was that no thought whatsoever could sustain him nor make him move. Once in front of the heavenly opening, he began to think and consider that someone could be coming. In his gaze, he saw the blessed Apostle Peter put his head through the opening with authority and a serious face, as if he wanted to say, *Clear the way. Make room and reverence for*

the coming of the Great King. Then he withdrew inside, after which, blessed Paul came, doing just like Peter, so that according to their request, Brother Roger made way for the coming of our Lord Jesus Christ, staying put, timid and full of reverence. After having seen these two apostles, Peter and Paul, both standing with great reverence, side by side, the Lord Jesus Christ came forth, like a priest leading his ministers in procession; and they passed in front of Brother Roger. Brother Roger started running after Christ and shouted very loudly, *Who are you Lord? Who are you?* In no way could he lift up his face higher than the knees of Christ, out of fear and awe. When he ran and shouted after him, Christ turned around and Brother Roger fell at his feet, shouting again with great joy, *Lord, who are you?* And Christ the Lord answered him, *I am the One Who Is,* and added, *Where do you come from my son?* He then blessed him with the sign of the cross, saying, *Your sins are remitted. Persevere in my grace and you will be with me for eternity.* After this, Brother Roger took courage and with one mighty effort looked Christ in the face for barely the time it takes for the twinkle of an eye. Thereafter, the image of the face of Christ was continually present to him whenever he thought about it. After this, he regained his former state. He told this to me and to many other confessors with such fervor and spirit that one could almost see him in the state in which he was when he saw these things." *Vita,* ch. 18, pp. 359–60.

17. *Vita,* ch. 20, p. 362.

18. Francis requires silence and discretion when it comes to God's revelations: "Blessed is the servant who, when he speaks, does not disclose everything about himself under the guise of a reward and is not quick to speak, but who is cautious about what he says" (*Admonition* 21); "Blessed is the servant who stores up in heaven the good things which the Lord shows to him and does not wish to reveal them to people under the guise of a reward, because the Most High Himself will reveal His deeds to whomever He wishes. Blessed is the servant who safeguards the secrets of the Lord in his heart" (*Admonition* 28), in *The Saint,* 135 and 137. For various accounts of the stigmata on Mount La Verna, see *The Life of Saint Francis* by Thomas of Celano (hereafter, 1C), ch. 3, 94–95, in *The Saint,* 263–65; *The Legend of Three Companions* (hereafter, L3C), ch. 17, 68–69, in *The Founder,* pp. 107–9; and *The Major Legend of Saint Francis* by Bonaventure of Bagnoreggio (hereafter, LMj), ch. 13, 3, in *The Founder,* pp. 630–39.

19. Giles's degrees of contemplation are found in ch. 13 of his *Golden Words.* His gift of ecstasy is reported in *Vita,* ch. 7, p. 352, in relation with Roger's degrees of "devotion": *cogitatio, amor, frequentatio, discretio, operatio, ostensio* and *remuneratio.* It is also significant that Roger's *Meditations*

THE EARLIEST FRANCISCANS

come right after Giles of Assisi's *Golden Words* in the *Avignon Compilation*.
See Paul Sabatier, "Compilation franciscaine d'Avignon," in *Revue d'Histoire
Franciscaine* 1 (1924): 425; hereafter, *RHF*.

20. See ChrXXIVG, AF, 3:393–406. The *Meditations* do not appear in
chapters, but in paragraphs. We have decided to number them from beginning to end.

21. The only indication of the friars is in *Meditation* 21, ChrXXIVG,
AF, 3:397: "And who is that lofty mountain, but you, Friar Minor? Look
carefully, then, to see if this is your life." Roger's work concerns all the friars, even if most meditations start with the second person singular of the
imperative mode, *considera* or *vide*. They address the friars' prayer life and
the steps needed to go to God. At times, the Friar Minor is also called "creature" or "miserable man."

22. See *RHF* 1 (1924): 425–31.

23. God's revelation to Moses at the burning bush: "I Am Who Am,"
Exod 3:14.

24. The Earlier Rule, ch. 23, 11, bears traces of the apophatic theology current. Francis speaks of God "without beginning and end, unchangeable, invisible, indescribable, ineffable, incomprehensible, unfathomable."
See *The Saint*, 86.

25. On the need for silence as opposed to frivolous words, see
Francis's *Admonitions* 20 and 21 in *The Saint*, 135; Giles's *Dicta*, ch. 17, pp.
58–59. The contempt for chattering and gossiping, useless words and
laughter goes back to Judeo-Christian and early monastic traditions. Saint
Benedict's Rule chastises the *verba otiosa*, *verba vana*, and *risus*. See *Saint
Benedict's Rule for Monasteries*, trans. by Leonard J. Doyle (Collegeville:
Liturgical Press, 2001), ch. 4, 51–54 and ch. 6, 8.

26. Certain *Meditations* seem triggered by Roger's ecstasies, where he
loses himself into God and identifies himself with God. This is obvious in
Meditations 4, 11, 14, 16, 18, 19, 27, and 28.

27. Roger of Provence's *Meditations* are labeled as a "spiritual work"
of the Middle Ages among the Franciscan theologians, preachers, and sym-
pathizers with the Spirituals. See Antonio Blasucci, "Auteurs spirituels au
14e siècle," in *Dictionnaire de Spiritualité*, vol. 5 (Paris: Beauchesne, 1964),
1342–43. Our English translation, from the Latin of the ChrXXIVG, AF,
3:393–406, is provided by Kathryn Krug. One can also find a much older
French translation in *Voie raccourcie de l'amour divin*, Textes recueillis et
traduits par Martial Lekeux (Paris: Lethielleux, 1957). An Italian translation is given in part by Cesare Vaiani, "Ruggero da Provenza," in *Dizionario
Francescano—I Mistici, secolo XIII*, vol. 1(Milano-Padova-Assisi: Edizioni
biblioteca Francescana-Ed. Messaggero-Ed. Porziuncola: 1995), 771–93. In

the notes, each *Meditation* is identified by its given number and the page in ChrXXIVG (as elsewhere throughout). Then, the reader will find the biblical references (exact quotes) and also the biblical and theological allusions used by Roger, followed at times by a short comment on the text.

28. *Meditation* 1, p. 393. References to Isa 3:10; Ps 76(77):12; and 1 Cor 2:10. There is also an allusion to Ps 7:9 and Rom 8:27 concerning God as assessor or expert in matters of the heart.

29. *Meditation* 2, p. 393. Reference to Ps 72(73):28. The reverence for God arouses reverence for humankind.

30. *Meditation* 3, p. 393. Allusions to Gen 1:26; 5:1; 9:6; and Col 3:10 where the human person is made in the likeness of God.

31. *Meditation* 4, pp. 393–94. References to Ps 15(16):11; Acts 2:28; and John 1:16. Allusion to God's declaration, "I Am Who Am," in Exod 3:14.

32. *Meditation* 5, p. 394. References to life as *a puff of smoke that disappears* in Jas 4:14, and the visible things that last for a time, in 2 Cor 4:18. The desire for the invisible is more important than any worldly thing.

33. *Meditation* 6, p. 394. Having access to prayer is a theme repeated in *Meditations* 38 and 39, like a spiritual transition leading to the vision of God.

34. *Meditation* 7, p. 394. References to Matt 6:21 or Luke 12:34. Allusion to Col 3:1ff with heavenly things and Christ at the right hand of God. Roger opposes the spiritual realm to being in exile, away from God.

35. *Meditation* 8, p. 394. Allusion to the Franciscan theme of body and flesh as vile, miserable, and like a form of leprosy.

36. *Meditation* 9, pp. 394–95. Allusion to Francis's *Admonition* 5, in *The Saint*, 131: "Consider, O human being, in what great excellence the Lord God has placed you, for He created and formed you to the image of His beloved Son according to the body and to His Likeness according to the Spirit." Also, allusion to Col 3:17. The *second way*, named here, is described in *Meditation* 4 as "the path of humanity by which we consider the things that are a human's in God."

37. *Meditation* 10, p. 395. Reference to Gal 6:17. Allusion to the hard human condition in Job 5:7.

38. *Meditation* 11, p. 395. Reference to John 1:5. Compare Augustine, *Confessions* 7, 10–16: "Nor will you change me into you, like the food of your flesh, but you will be changed into me," *Augustine of Hippo: Selected Writings*, trans. Mary T. Clark (New York: Paulist Press, 1984), 71.

39. *Meditation* 12, p. 395. References to Prov 13:12. Allusion to Ps 35(36):8–9 and the notion of pleasure.

40. *Meditation* 13, pp. 395–96. First mention of the sweetness of heaven. "In via" (on the way) is another way of rendering the idea of exile;

it expresses the ongoing journey of humankind as opposed to the definitive state in which dwell the angels and the blessed. There is also an allusion to the kindness and tenderness of God as found in Ps 68(69):15–16.

41. *Meditation* 14, p. 396. Reference to Prov 8:31. This consideration is a consequence of Roger's ecstasies. He considers spiritual union as a radical experience where one is in God and God is in one's soul.

42. *Meditation* 15, p. 396. Roger repeats the Augustinian notion of "fruition" echoed in the Franciscan tradition, and beforehand, in the Cistercian tradition. See St. Augustine, *On Christian Doctrine*, ch. 33, n. 37. A possible source for "tasting the Spirit" is in St. Bernard, *Letter* 111, n. 3: *Gustato spiritu, necesse est desipere carnem*, (cf. *Opere di San Bernardo*, vol. VI/1, *Lettere* 1–120). For the Franciscan tradition, see St. Bonaventure, *I Sent. Dist.* 1, a.3, q.1 where one finds the same affirmation: *Deo fruendum est*.

43. *Meditation* 16, p. 396. Roger's notion of the presence of God and his omniscience not only concerns the things of the past, the present, and the future but also the things that could have happened and did not.

44. *Meditation* 17, pp. 396–97. Reference to Rom 11:33.

45. *Meditation* 18, p. 397. Reference to Ps 99(100):3.

46. *Meditation* 19, p. 397.

47. *Meditation* 20, p. 397. Roger evokes the struggle between intellect and affect, two forces of the soul, a theme often disputed between Franciscans and Dominicans. The expression *nauseant super cibo* is an allusion to the Israelites' complaining about the desert manna as "wretched food," Num 21:5.

48. *Meditation* 21, p. 397. References to Matt 4:4 or Luke 4:4 and Deut 8:3.

49. *Meditation* 22, p. 398.

50. *Meditation* 23, p. 398. Allusion to Ps 21(22):6: "Yet here I am, now more worm than man" (Jerusalem Bible, 1968).

51. *Meditation* 24, p. 398. Reference to Luke 17:10.

52. *Meditation* 25, p. 398. Reference to Ps 106(107):10 and Luke 1:79. The world is seen as a solemn feast; his description of God's solemn celebration through the elements of creation expresses Roger's connection to nature mysticism.

53. *Meditation* 26, p. 398. Allusion to Christ's offering for the world in Heb 7:27. Reference to Matt 27:51.

54. *Meditation* 27, p. 399. Allusion to the listeners of the Gospel who listen without hearing, in Matt 13:15.

55. *Meditation* 28, p. 399. Latin: *Qui sibi ipsi Deus est*. The entire consideration refers to being in God, having passed over into God, and living totally in him.

56. *Meditation* 29, p. 399. Allusion to Rom 8:20, where creation retains the hope of being freed by God. Here is another evocation of the world of nature or creation. Roger seems to have been influenced by Francis's *Canticle of the Creatures*. See *The Saint*, 113–14.

57. *Meditation* 30, pp. 399–400. Another allusion to Gen 1:26 and humankind created in the likeness of God.

58. *Meditation* 31, p. 400. Reference to Ps 33(34):6.

59. *Meditation* 32, p. 400–401. Reference to Ps 63(64):7. Here is a conversation between *anima* and *caro*. Roger's use of bitterness and sweetness recalls Francis's experience of conversion in his *Testament*. See *The Saint*, 124. This text reveals a strong desire for death in order to love God totally. Ps 63(64):7–8, translated here as Roger quotes it, according to the older Vulgate (*Accedet homo ad cor altum et exaltabitur Deus*), is very different in newer versions. In the 1945 Vulgate, we have *Et mens cuiusque et cor sunt profunda. Sed Deus ferit eos sagittis*: "Deep are the thoughts of each heart. But God shoots his arrows at them" (New American Bible [NAB]).

60. *Meditation* 33, p. 401. Reference to Gen 1:31 and allusion to Ps 141(142):8: "Lead me forth from prison, that I may give thanks to your name" (NAB).

61. *Meditation* 34, pp. 401–2. Reference to 2 Cor 3:18. On intimacy with God and knowing God interiorly, see Bonaventure quoting St. Augustine in *Opera Omnia*, 8:31n3. Also allusion to knowing God from experience, in Alvarus Pelagius, *De Planctu Ecclesiae*, vol. 2, ch. 93. This entire meditation reveals Roger's mystical experience of elevation.

62. *Meditation* 35, p. 402. Innovative way of speaking of silence, both exterior and interior: silence as revealer of God's own silence.

63. *Meditation* 36, p. 402. In trying to give an explanation to the expression "whose soul, in God, knows what it is to become God" (*cuius in Deo anima fieri novit Deus*), the editors add in a footnote, *non substantialiter, sed unitive et transformative*. Roger, therefore, speaks of transformation and union in God. He also invents the Latin word *ingustus*, "not-tasted," to render the concept of nonfeeling. This entire meditation reveals the notion of mystical inexpressibility.

64. *Meditation* 37, pp. 402–3. Reference to 2 Cor 1:3 and Ps 24(25):6. Here is a rare statement on love of neighbor leading to love of God. This entire meditation is not clear, which makes our translation difficult. Even the *Analecta Franciscana* editors observe that certain sentences are "corrupt and obscure."

65. *Meditation* 38, p. 403. Here again the text is obscure, yet evokes the soul's identification with God, as seen already in *Meditations* 28 and 36.

66. *Meditation* 39, p. 403. Roger names various spiritual steps briefly. He develops them much more in *Meditation* 40.

67. *Meditation* 40, pp. 403–4. Allusion to Ps 18(19):5 and the tent in the splendor of the sun. References to Ps 45(46):11; Deut 32:39; Job 14:4; Jer 51:19; Exod 3:14; Ps 30(31):17. Allusions to John 1:5 and the light that could not be overpowered by the darkness and Jer 33:5 and the conversion of Jerusalem. In the strange *jubilus* finale of the meditation, Roger tries to find words to match his ecstatic admiration of the ineffability and inexpressibility of God as the *One Who Is*, in the biblical sense.

James of Milan

1. The second half of the thirteenth century as a time period for James's life is found in the preface of the second critical edition of the *Stimulus Amoris*: "Unde fr. Iacobum in secunda saeculi XIII parte vixisse deducimus." The *Stimulus* thus becomes the direct source for James's life. See *Stimulus Amoris Fr. Iacobi Mediolanensis. Canticum Pauperis Fr. Ioannis Peckam*, Bibliotheca Franciscana Ascetica Medii Aevi 4 (Quaracchi: Collegium S. Bonaventurae, 1905 and 1949): p. x of the 1949 edition; hereafter, *Stimulus*.

2. Salimbene, *Chronica Fratris Salimbene de Adam Ordinis Minorum*, ed. O. Holder-Egger (MGH/Scriptorum [Hanover: 1905–13] 32), 390: "Dicebant autem michi duo fratres Minores de Mediolano, qui cum legato manebant, scilicet fr. Iacobus et fr. Gregorius." For a basic introduction to James of Milan, see Clément Schmitt, "Jacques de Milan," *Catholicisme* 6 (1963): 279; Pierre Péano, "Jacques de Milan," in *Dictionnaire de Spiritualité*, vol. 8 (1972), 48–49; John V. Fleming, *An Introduction to the Franciscan Literature of the Middle Ages* (Chicago: Franciscan Herald Press, 1977), 214–15; Ilarino da Milano, "Giacomo da Milano," *Enciclopedia Cattolica* 6 (1951): 328–29; Bernard McGinn, *The Flowering of Mysticism: Men and Women in the New Mysticism—1200–1350* (New York: Crossroad Herder, 1998), 118 and 380; hereafter, McGinn, *Flowering*.

3. Bartholomew of Pisa, *De Conformitate vitae beati Francisci ad vitam Domini Iesu*, Analecta Franciscana 4 (1906): 341; hereafter, *De Conformitate*, AF, vol. 4.

4. On his relocation to Domodossola, see Celestino Piana, "Il 'Fr. Iacobus de Mediolano lector' autore dello pseudo-bonaventuriano *Stimulus Amoris* ed un convento del suo insegnamento," *Antonianum* 61 (1986): 329–39. The interpretation of James's "demotion" and move to

Domodossola because of his association with the Spirituals comes from Maria Pia Alberzoni, "'L'approbatio': Curia romana, Ordine minoritico e Liber," in *Angela de Foligno: le dossier*, Collection de l'École Française de Rome 255, ed. Giulia Barone and Jacques Dalarun (Rome: École Française, 1999), 312–14. Alberzoni also advances the hypothesis that James could have been one of the lectors who signed the *approbatio* of Angela of Foligno's *Memorial* and notes some of the *Memorial*'s similarities with the spirituality of the *Stimulus Amoris*, 314. For a possible association between the *Stimulus* and the Gugliemites, a popular heresy, see Stephen E. Wessley, "James of Milan and the Gugliemites: Franciscan Spirituality and Popular Heresy in Late Thirteenth Century Italy," *Collectanea Francescana* 54 (1984): 6–20.

5. For an excellent presentation of the debate between the Spiritual Franciscans and the Community, including discussion of the opposition between the Franciscan leadership and the papacy of the time, see David Burr, *The Spiritual Franciscans* (University Park: Pennsylvania State University Press, 2001).

6. Hilton's translation has been edited by Harold Kane, *The Prickynge of Love*, 2 vols. (Salzburg: Institut für Anglistik und Amerikanistik, 1983). See also Walter Hilton, *The Goad of Love: An Unpublished Translation of the Stimulus Amoris, Formerly Attributed to Saint Bonaventure*, ed. Clare Kirchberger (London: Faber and Faber, 1952). In her introduction to Hilton's *Goad of Love*, Kirchberger remarks that Hilton tones down James of Milan's *Stimulus*, cancelling entire passages of extreme devotion, and thus eliminating many evocations of mystical union. It seems Hilton had a purpose: he wanted to skip any abstract vocabulary reminiscent of Pseudo-Dionysius, the Victorines, and the *Cloud of Unknowing*; they had caused confusion and many heretical errors in the thirteenth and fourteenth centuries. Translations in other languages are listed in n29.

7. Manuscript 10, *Bibliothecae Mediceae Laurentianae*, 19.

8. *De Conformitate*, AF, 4:341.

9. The original version of the *Stimulus* contains two full chapters devoted to meditation on the Passion, and the theme also occurs elsewhere; the longer version from the later fourteenth century has fifteen chapters on the Passion. For a thorough history of the manuscript tradition and its dissemination, see the doctoral thesis of Falk Eisermann, *'Stimulus amoris': Inhalt, lateinische Überlieferung, deutsche Übersetzungen, Rezeption* (Tübingen: Max Niemeyer, 2001), 1, 4, and 212. See also Kathryn Krug, "James of Milan's *Stimulus Amoris*: Through the Wounds to the Womb of Christ," paper presented on May 14, 2010, at the Forty-Fifth International Congress on Medieval Studies, Kalamazoo, Michigan; Silvia Mostaccio,

"Giacomo da Milano," in *Dizionario Biografico degli Italiani*, vol. 54 (Rome: Treccani, 2000), 222; Thomas H. Besbul, *Texts of the Passion: Latin Devotional Literature and Medieval Society* (Philadelphia: University of Pennsylvania Press, 1906), 56.

10. As edited by the Quaracchi Franciscans, in the 1949 revised edition. See n1.

11. *Stimulus*, prologue, p. 2. In the prologue, James also calls his brother John, *Eucharis*, as opposed to himself, *Supplantatore*, referring to the biblical twins Jacob, the "Supplantor" (the deceiver) and Esau (his *blessed* hairy brother).

12. *Stimulus*, ch. 12, p. 57: "For we do not want to yield to the will of our superiors, but wish that our desires should be fulfilled in everything....For we do not consider how we can more fully carry out their will and more perfectly deny our own desires."

13. *Stimulus*, ch. 16, p. 84.

14. See Casimir Oudin, *Commentarius de scriptoribus ecclesiae antiquis illorumque scriptis*, vol. 3, Leipzig, 1722, col. 422–24.

15. *Stimulus*, ch. 18, p. 113.

16. *Stimulus*, prologue, p. 3.

17. Kathryn Krug (see n9) observes in her Kalamazoo paper (p. 2): "Throughout the book, there is a mixture of writing in the first, second, and third person; thus the work switches, easily and continually, along a range of the personal, didactic, intimately prayerful, and expository."

18. The chapters in the *forma brevis* range in size from a single paragraph to ten (pocket-sized) pages. The variety of topics can be gleaned from the chapter titles, given with the translation below.

19. *Stimulus*, prologue, pp. 3–5. The Latin *vulnus* in the phrase *vulnere amoris tui* means wounds, much more drastic than the word *goad*. Christ's wounds are not superficial; they pierce him through, fixing him to the cross. They also suggest the soul's effort to take refuge in them. This call to enter into the wounds of Christ and dwell in them is a recurring motif of medieval meditations. The *Stimulus* exploits the theme of the wounds of Christ in chapters 1 (p. 13), 3 (p. 17), 6 (pp. 29–30), 7 (pp. 32–35), 14 (pp. 71–75), 15 (pp. 78–81), 16 (p. 93), 19 (p. 116), and 23 (p. 129).

20. For the theme of the Passion of Christ in medieval devotion, see Richard Kieckhefer, "Devotion to the Passion," in *Unquiet Souls: Fourteenth-Century Saints in Their Religious Milieu* (Chicago: University of Chicago Press, 1984), 89–121.

21. For instance, in one of his letters, Angelo Clareno, one of the leaders of the Spirituals, affirms, "This is the life and the rule of the disciples of Christ: deny one's own body, soul, senses, and will; and faith and

obedience consists in the need, for the sake of Christ, to fervently desire suffering, insults, a bitter death, and shamefulness." Letter 64 in *Angeli Clareni Opera. I, Epistole*, ed. Lydia Von Auw (Rome: Nella Sede dell'Istituto Palazzo Borromini, 1980), 300, cited by Gian Luca Potestà, "Ideali di santità secondo Ubertino da Casale ed Angelo Clareno," in *Santi e santità nel secolo XIV*, Atti del XV Convegno Internazionale, Assisi, 15–17 October 1987 (Rome: Edizioni Scientifiche Italiane, 1989), 312–13.

22. *Stimulus*, ch. 18, pp. 109–10.

23. *Stimulus*, ch. 23, pp. 126–27: reference to Matt 26:41.

24. *Stimulus*, ch. 23, p. 129.

25. See Carolyn Walker Bynum, "Jesus as Mother and Abbot as Mother: Some Themes in Twelfth-Century Cistercian Writings," in *Jesus as Mother: Studies in the Spirituality of the High Middle Ages* (Berkeley: University of California Press, 1982), 110–69. On this theme, see also Barbara Newman, *God and the Goddesses: Vision, Poetry, and Belief in the Middle Ages* (Philadelphia: University of Pennsylvania Press, 2003), 190–234.

26. *Angela of Foligno, Complete Works*, ed. and trans. Paul Lachance (New York: Paulist Press, 1993), 139–40. See also Ingrid Peterson, "Angela of Foligno: The Active Life and the Following of Christ," *Studies in Spirituality* 10 (2000): 125–41; "Images of the Crucified Christ in Clare of Assisi and Angela of Foligno," in *That Others May Know and Love: Essays in Honor of Zachary Hayes, o.f.m.*, ed. Michael Cusato and Edward Coughlin (St. Bonaventure, NY: Franciscan Institute, 1997), 167–92; and "Angela of Foligno (1248–1305)," in *The Franciscan Tradition*, ed. by Regis Armstrong and Ingrid Peterson (Collegeville, MI: Liturgical Press, 2010), 110–17.

27. Free translation of Jerome Poulenc, OFM, "Saint François dans le 'vitrail des anges' de l'église supérieure de la basilique d'Assise," *Archivum Franciscanum Historicum* 76 (1983): 703.

28. In an insightful study on the social function and imaginative effects of the imagery of the crucified Christ in medieval devotion, Sarah Beckwith, commenting on this text, makes the following observation: "As well as functioning as breast, the wound at Christ's side is a womb in the act of perpetual parturition....Here the acknowledgment that Christ's body is welcomingly open almost immediately sponsors the anxiety that the very openness of the wounds will not allow them to provide a safe harbouring place for the soul. If the wounds are too open they cannot retain and protect the soul they sequester; if they are too closed there would, in this scenario, be no point of entry for the soul in the first place. The fantasy, then, that it provides for this dilemma is one of perpetual parturition, an ensured

birthing and re-birthing which guarantees that the relationship between the inside and outside of Christ's body will permit the passage of the ardent soul. In James of Milan's *Stimulus Amoris* the original pun between *vulnus* and *vulva* makes the equation an even more grotesquely economical one. The image is one of a parturition that can never be finished, so that the wounds can stay open around the infant soul. And the regression to a foetus-like comfort can keep open the boundaries between inside and outside. We might say that one of the functions of the wounds in this text is to melt all dividing differences....The boundaries of Christ's body and the body of the devotee are made so soft and so continuous with each other that where one ends and where the other begins become indeterminable." See Sara Beckwith, *Christ's Body: Identity, Culture and Society in Late Medieval Writings* (New York: Routledge, 1993), 55–62; hereafter, Beckwith, *Christ's Body*.

29. Our English translation by Kathryn Krug comes from the critical edition of the Quaracchi Franciscans, mentioned in n1. McGinn, *Flowering*, 118 mentions several translations: Italian, French, Spanish, German, English, and even Gaelic. For instance, *L'aiguillon d'amour. Traité d'ascétisme longtemps attribué à saint Bonaventure*, translated by Ubald d'Alençon (Paris–Couvin: Ancienne Librairie Poussielgue—Maison Saint-Roch, 1910); *The Goad of Love*, now edited from manuscripts by Clare Kirchberger; *Love's Prompting by James of Milan*, translated by Campion Murray (ebook available online, http://sfo.franciscans.org.au/sfo13/Love's %20Prompting/Love's%20Prompting.doc); *Lo Stimolo del divino amore*, translated by Cesare Guasti (Milano: V&P, 1945); A. Levasti, ed., *I mistici del Duecento e del Trecento* (Milan: Rizzoli, 1935). See also Kane, cited in n6, above.

30. *Stimulus*, prologue, pp. 3–5; references to Ps 83(84):3, Phil 1:23, Wis 16:20–21. The long quotation comes from Bonaventure, *Soliloquium*, c. 1, n. 18.

31. *Stimulus*, ch. 1, pp. 7–8, 9, and 13; reference to 1 Tim 6:15. Chapter 1 offers ten rules of spiritual growth for a person eager to please God. There is a Franciscan tone in James's vocabulary, the practice of Christian virtues, and nonjudgment toward other people's sins. The theme of the wounded heart of Christ as source of grace, found here, in the opening prayer, and throughout the *Stimulus*, is part of a rich tradition of devotion to the Sacred Heart. According to Eller, "The transition from the patristic theology of the wounded side of Christ as the Source of Grace, to the medieval pastoral preaching of special devotion to the Heart of Christ was a gradual one. The devotion was divulged rapidly: *implicit* in Francis's adherence to the Humanity of Christ, to the wounds of Christ; *implicit* also

in the *Sermons* of Anthony; and then shortly thereafter *explicit* in the works of the Doctor Seraphicus, Bonaventure." See Hugh Eller, "James of Milan and the Stimulus Amoris," in *Franciscan Christology*, ed. Damian McElrath (St. Bonaventure, NY: Franciscan Institute Publications, 1980), 90. See also L. di Fonzo and G. Colassanti, "Il culto del Sacro Cuore negli Ordini Francescani," in *Cor Jesu, Commentationes in Litteras Encyclicas PP. XII*, "Haurietis Aquas," vol. 2, ed. A. Bea, K. Rahner, H. Rondet, and F. Schwendimann (Rome: Herder, 1959), 99–137.

32. *Stimulus*, ch. 2, p. 14; references to Ps 72(73):1, Wis 12:1.

33. *Stimulus*, ch. 3, pp. 15–18.

34. *Stimulus*, ch. 4, p. 2; reference to Song 2:6. From chapters 4 to 9, James shows the different paths that send a person into rapture.

35. *Stimulus*, ch. 5, pp. 26–27. Chapter 5 is close to St. Francis's theme of *redditio*, in his *Admonitions*.

36. *Stimulus*, ch. 6, pp. 28–29; reference to 2 Sam 17:19.

37. *Stimulus*, ch. 7, pp. 33–34.

38. *Stimulus*, ch. 8, pp. 38–39. Chapter 8 recalls the love relationship between the soul and God in the *Song of Songs*.

39. *Stimulus*, ch. 9, pp. 40–41. McGinn notes that chapter 9 "distinguishes between an *inebriatio…in intensione laetitiae* achieved through compassion with Christ on the cross, which is primarily in the heart, but which also finds external expression, and an *inebriatio…in intensione dulcedinis*, which reduces the soul to sleep or quiet in which all sense activity is taken away." Since temptation can imitate the latter, James warns "to beware of pride and to fix the eyes of the spirit on God alone." See McGinn, *Flowering*, 381n32.

40. *Stimulus*, ch. 10, pp. 44–47. Chapter 10 develops the *bitter/sweet* theme of St. Francis's conversion, as seen in his *Testament*. Chapters 10 to 15 name the many responsibilities of a contemplative.

41. *Stimulus*, ch. 11, pp. 50–53; references to Neh 4:17, Job 28:25.

42. *Stimulus*, ch. 12, pp. 56–61.

43. *Stimulus*, ch. 13, pp. 63–64.

44. *Stimulus*, ch. 14, pp. 70–73; references Matt 17:4, Hos 2:14 (2:16 in the New American Bible), Luke 2:35. McGinn calls the mixing of the Virgin's milk with the blood of Christ a "baroque mystical conceit." McGinn, *Flowering*, 380n30.

45. In Latin, this is a series of almost-rhyming wordplays, hence adding musicality to the text: *Non vulgus, sed vulnus; non pressuram, sed fixuram; non clamorem, sed livorem; non horrorem, sed dolorem.*

46. *Stimulus*, ch. 15, pp. 77–82; references to John 19:25, Lam 1:20.

47. *Stimulus*, ch. 16, pp. 83–93. Chapters 16 to 23 develop the atti-

tudes toward God and one's neighbor that one needs in order to be completely transformed into God.

48. *Stimulus*, ch. 17, pp. 94–95.

49. *Stimulus*, ch. 18, pp. 105–114. For a passage from ch. 18, see the section "Structure and Content" in this chapter's introduction.

50. *Stimulus*, ch. 19, pp. 115–16; reference to Ps 76(77):11.

51. *Stimulus*, ch. 20, pp. 118–19.

52. *Stimulus*, ch. 21, pp. 120–22.

53. *Stimulus*, ch. 22, pp. 123–25. Chapter 22 has a close kinship with a theme dear to St. Francis, that of *word and deed*.

54. *Stimulus*, ch. 23, pp. 128–29. For other passages of ch. 23, see section "Structure and Content" in the introduction.

General Conclusion

1. Francis of Assisi, *Admonition XVI* in *The Saint*, 134.

2. *Meditation*, 39.

3. See Bernard McGinn, *The Foundations of Mysticism—Origins to the Fifth Century* (New York: Crossroad, 1991) vol. 1, general introduction, pp. xi–xx.

4. *Stimulus amoris*, ch. 14, p. 72.

5. On that subject, see Luigi Pellegrini, *Insediamenti francescani nell'Italia del Duecento* (Rome: Ed. Laurentianum, 1984).

6. *Golden Sayings*, ch. 15.

SELECT BIBLIOGRAPHY

1. Primary Texts, Latin and English

Angelo Clareno. *A Chronicle or History of the Seven Tribulations of the Order of Brothers Minor*. Translated by David Burr and E. Randolph Daniel. St. Bonaventure, NY. Franciscan Institute Publications, 2005.

Arnaud of Sarrant. "Meditationes fratris Rogerii supradicti Provincialis." *Analecta Franciscana sive Chronica Aliaque Varia Documenta ad Historiam Fratrum Minorum*, vol. 3, 393–406. Quaracchi. Collegium S. Bonaventurae, 1877.

Dicta Beati aegidii Assisiensis. Bibliotheca Franciscana Ascetica Medii aevi, vol. 3. Edited by Gisbert Menge, OFM. Quaracchi. Collegium S. Bonaventurae, 1905.

Francis of Assisi: Early Documents. Edited by Regis Armstrong, OFM Cap., A. Wayne Hellmann, OFM Conv., and William Short, OFM. Hyde Park, NY. New City Press, 2000. Vol. 1, *The Saint*; Vol. 2, *The Founder*; Vol. 3, *The Prophet*.

The Prickynge of Love. Edited by Harold Kane. 2 vols. Salzburg: Institut für Anglistik und Amerikanistik, 1983.

Raymond Petri. "De venerabili frater Rogerio, O.S.Fr." *Codicum Hagiographicum Bibliothecae Regiae Bruxellensis*, Par. I. Codices Latini Membranei, vol. 1. Ediderunt Hagiographi Bollandiani. Brussels. Analecta Bollandiana, 1886.

Scripta Leonis, Rufini et Angeli sociorum S. Francisci: The Writings of Leo, Rufino and Angelo, Companions of St. Francis. Edited and translated by Rosalind B. Brooke. Oxford. Clarendon Press, 1970.

Stimulus Amoris Fr. Iacobi Mediolanensis. Canticum Pauperis Fr. Ioannis Peckam. Bibliotheca Franciscana Ascetica Medii Aevi, vol. 4. Quaracchi. Collegium S. Bonaventurae, 1905 and 1949.

Walter Hilton. *The Goad of Love: An Unpublished Translation of the Stimulus Amoris Formerly Attributed to St. Bonaventure.* Edited by Clare Kircheberger. London: Faber & Faber, 1951.

2. Select Secondary Studies

Beckwith, Sarah. *Christ's Body: Identity, Culture, and Society in Late Medieval Writings.* New York: Routledge, 1993.

Brown, Raphael. *Franciscan Mystic: The Life of Blessed Brother Giles of Assisi, Companion of St. Francis.* Garden City, NY: Hanover House, 1962.

Brufani, Stefano. "Egidio d'Assisi: un santità feriale." *I compagni di Francesco e la prima generazione minoritica*, 285–311. Spoleto: Centro Italiano di Studi sull'alto medioevo, 1992.

Burr, David. *The Spiritual Franciscans.* University Park: Pennsylvania State University Press, 2001.

Cambell, Jacques. "Giles d'Assise." *Dictionnaire de spiritualité.* Vol. 6, 379–82. Paris: Beauchesne, 1937–94.

Carozzi, Claude. "Extases et visions chez frère Roger de Provence." *Fin du monde et signes de temps: Visonnaires et prophètes en France méridionale* (fin XIIIe–début XVe siècle), 81–105. Toulouse: Privat, 1976.

Clark, J. P. H. "Walter Hilton and the Stimulus Amoris." *Downside Review* 101 (1983): 79–118.

Da Campagnola, Stanislao. "Le 'Legenda' di frate Edigio d'Assisi nei secoli XIII–XV." *Francescanesimo e società cittadina. L'esempio di Perugia (1276–1976).* Edited by Ugolino Nicolini, 113–43. Spoleto: Centro Italiano di Studi sull'alto medioevo, 1979.

Dizionario Francescano. I Mistici. Secolo XIII. Bologna: Editrici Francescane, 1995.

Eisermann, Falk. *'Stimulus amoris': Inhalt, laterinische Überlieferung, deutsche Übersetzungen, Rezeption.* Tübingen: Max Niemeyer, 2001.

Eller, Hugh. "James of Milan and the Stimulus Amoris." In *Franciscan Christology*, edited by Damian McElroth, 89–107. St. Bonaventure, NY: Franciscan Publications, 1980.

Fortini, Arnaldo. *Francis of Assisi.* New York. Crossroad, 1981.

Le Goff, Jacques. "The Wilderness in Medieval West." *The Medieval Imagination.* Chicago. University of Chicago Press, 1988.

Mariani, Eliodoro. *La Sapienza di frate Egidio compagno di San Francesco con I Detti.* Vicenza: LIEF, 1981.

McGinn, Bernard. *The Flowering of Mysticism: Men and Women in the New Mysticism—1200-1350.* New York. Crossroad, 1998.

Moorman, John. *A History of the Franciscan Order: From its Origins to the Year 1517.* Oxford: Clarendon Press, 1968.

Péano, Pierre. "Jacques de Milan." *Dictionnaire de spiritualité.* Vol. 8, 48–49.

Piana, Celestino. "Il 'Fr. Iacobus de Mediolano Lector' autore dello Pseudo-Bonaventuriano Stimulus Amoris ed un convento del suo insegnamento." *Antonianum* 61 (1986): 329–39.

Ruh, Kurt. *Geschichte der abendländische Mystik.* Band. II, section XXV. *Frauenmystik und Franziskanische Mystik der Frühzeit.* Munich. C. H. Beck, 1993.

Théry, Gabriel. "Thomas Gallus et Egide d'Assise. Le 'De Septem Gradibus Contemplationis." *Revue Néo-Scholastique de Philosophie* 36 (1934): 180–90.

Wessley, Stephen. "James of Milan and the Guglielmites: Franciscan Spirituality and Popular Heresy in Late Thirteenth-Century Milan." *Collectanea Francescana* 54 (1984): 5–20.

INDEX